It is uncommon for one book to provide both robust theory along with practical applications on any subject matter, but this is one of those uncommon books. The authors manage to provide the theoretical underpinnings of a child's need for attachment while providing practical guidance to courts, social workers, agencies and families on how to achieve it. Bravo! (Mark Bontrager, Executive Director, Aldea Children and Family Services, Napa, CA)

No one is more knowledgeable or experienced in the child welfare arena than Jim Kenny and Lori Groves who clearly epitomize how the courts and law makers can most effectively prevent trauma to children facing the loss of their bonded families. *Bonding and the Case for Permanence* should be a mandatory read for decision makers and attorneys appointed to be the voice of children. (Debbie Grabarkiewicz, Child Advocacy Specialist, A Child's Best Interest, Ann Arbor, MI)

This book is clearly written by an "insider" to the system, albeit an insider with a degree in psychology whose ear is most finely attuned to the needs of foster children. *Bonding and the Case for Permanence* is that "wise mentor" for true child advocates in the foster care system. Good work / God's work. (Marguerite Rebesco, PhD, Clinical Psychologist)

It is the rare piece of work that gives equal weight to the importance of bonding and permanence at both ends of our foster care system. *Bonding and a Case for Permanence* is one of the best guides out there for all the stakeholders in our field including foster parents. The authors not only make an effective case for the importance of bonding and permanence for all children entering foster care but they make an equally extraordinary case for permanence for all youth and young adults exiting foster care as well. Excellent Job! (Pat O'Brien, Executive Director, You Gotta Believe! New York, NY)

The authors have done their homework sifting through the literature. The result is a clear and practical mandate for action to ensure that a child's right to safety, security and permanency are seen as a *crisis of need as serious as any hospitalization in intensive care* once he enters the system. (Cynthia Peck, author, editor, foster and adoptive parent)

Bonding is critical to the well-being of a child and there is ample evidence that shows the negative consequences that can occur when bonding is disrupted. Every child deserves a stable, permanent home. This book describes the importance of achieving this goal within a reasonable period of time. The reader will be enlightened, and those working in the child welfare, foster care, and adoption arenas will find the book especially valuable. (Michael Patchner, Dean, IU School of Social Work)

Kenny and Groves fill a gaping hole in understanding and dealing with a most serious consequence of trauma. This book should be required reading for ANYONE who works with youth, and especially those youth in foster care – similar to the ethical equivalent of the oath "Do No Harm." (Christina Morrison, Executive Director, Indiana Foster Care and Adoption Association, Inc.)

As the editor of Fostering Families Today, I know that reprints of the authors' articles on bonding have been requested more than any others. As foster parents prepare to battle in court to adopt the children they have come to love and cherish, there is no better support than the authors' definition of bonding and the listing of court battles won on the concept of bonding trumping biology. Now, those parents will have all of the authors' wisdom in one place, the new book, *Bonding and the Case for Permanence.* (Kim Phagan-Hansel, Editor of *Fostering Families Today*)

BONDING AND THE CASE FOR PERMANENCE

PREVENTING MENTAL ILLNESS, CRIME, AND HOMELESSNESS AMONG CHILDREN IN FOSTER CARE AND ADOPTION

A GUIDE FOR ATTORNEYS, JUDGES, THERAPISTS AND CHILD WELFARE

James Kenny, PhD, and Lori Groves, BA

ACT PUBLCATIONS, PO Box 318, Rensselaer, IN 47978

2010

ISBN 1451593538
EAN-13 9781451593532

TABLE OF CONTENTS

INTRODUCTION:

Bonding Is a Critical Issue   1

PART ONE: THE PROBLEM   5

1. **BROKEN PROMISES   7**
   How We Break Our Promise   8
   The Child's Rights Are Paramount   10
   The Rights of the Child   10
   The Pain of Waiting   14
   Why We Break Our Promise   15

2. **WHAT EVERYONE NEEDS TO KNOW ABOUT BONDING   19**
   Definition of Terms   20
   Attachment   21
   A History of Bonding Definitions   24
   Bonding Defined   26
   What Bonding Is Not   32
   Bonding Myths   33
   How Bonding Develops   37
   Sibling Bonding   39
   Multiple Attachments or Bonds   42
   Conclusion   42

3. **THE HIGH PRICE OF INSTABILITY   45**
   The Consequences of Separation and Loss   46
   What Happens When Bonding Is Interrupted?   47
   Why Children Are Moved   53
   Emancipation to Independent Living   54
   Statements of Fact   57

PART TWO: THE HARM DONE BY FAILURE TO PROVIDE PERMANENCE   59

4. **DELAY, DESPAIR, AND DETACHMENT: THE PHYSICAL AND MENTAL HEALTH OF FOSTER CHILDREN   61**
   From Delay to Despair   62
   Childhood Mental Illness   63
   Adult Mental Illness   67

5. STRIKING BACK IN ANGER: DELINQUENCY AND CRIME IN
   FOSTER CHILDREN   71
6. NO PLACE TO CALL HOME: MOVING TOWARD HOMELESSNESS
   77
   Foster Care Runaways   77
   Homelessness   78
7. THE CHALLENGE   81
   The Systems Are Failing   81
   Reasons for Delay   83
   The Players   84
   Cooperative Adoption   86

PART THREE: WHAT THE MAJOR PLAYERS CAN DO   89

8. WHAT FOSTER/ADOPT PARENTS CAN DO   91
   A Permanent Home   91
   Preparing a Life Book   92
   Keeping a Journal   95
   Modeling Attachment   97
   A Voice for Foster Parents   101
9. THE ROLE OF THE MENTAL HEALTH PROFESSIONAL   105
   Diagnosis   105
   Treating Reactive Attachment Disorder   106
   The Assessment of Bonding   111
10. HOW THE CHILD WELFARE DEPARTMENT CAN HELP   117
    Recommended Policy Changes   118
    Caseworkers can make a Difference   120

PART FOUR: GOING TO COURT   123

11. COURTS HAVE THE FINAL WORD   125
    Presenting Bonding in Court   125
    Hiring an Attorney   125
    The Attorney's Role   126
    Bonding Must Be Clearly Defined   128
    Expert Testimony: The Mental Health Professional as Witness   131
    The Foster/Adopt Parent as Witness   132
    The Role of the CASA/GAL   133
    The Court has Problems   134

12. THE RIGHT TO A PERMANENT HOME   137

The Journey of the Foster Child   137
Pseudo-Permanency Plans   139
Conclusions   140

APPENDICES   143

A. Summary of the Adoption and Safe Families Act of 1997   145
B. Summary of the Fostering Connections and Increasing Adoptions Act   153
C. Appellate Court Decisions Favoring Bonding   159
D. Quarterly Summary for Case Conferences and Court Hearings   167
E. Initial Plan for Family Reunification   171
F. Groves Bonding Checklist   173
G. Daily Journal for Foster Parents   177

REFERENCES   179

BONDING IS A CRITICAL ISSUE

When two items are attached with crazy glue, they are bonded. Pulling them apart is very difficult. Separation is possible but at some considerable cost. Parts of both sides may be ripped apart. The result is ugly.

Bonding between humans shares this quality. Bonds are tight and they are broken at the considerable risk of harming both sides. Bonding is a stronger term than attachment. Much more than attachment, bonding has a tenacious sticking quality. One breaks or violates a bond at a high price. The severance of a bond is more critical to the child's well-being than many have allowed.

Relationships are essential to the human condition. We need some degree of trust and intimacy with our fellows. Failure to develop intimate ties deprives us of personal growth and the capacity to perceive the needs of others as our own. No one is self-sufficient. We all need one another. Bonding is vital for survival and our sense of self.

Our connection to other humans, especially to our parents and siblings, shapes our development. Our self-image is fashioned in good part by the way that we imagine we are perceived. Children internalize and view themselves in accord with how they are treated.

Children depend on adults for nurture and survival. Children who have suffered significant loss may see no safe options. To a child, love and bonding mean safety. They have no lasting experience with separation. Each loss becomes global and forever, a dire prophecy of what will happen in the future. The child may decide: "It hurts to count on others. No

1

one will ever love me. I will never again let myself get this close to anyone."

Early and repeated loss of a bonded and loved parent may cause a child to pull back, to guard against any future attachments. A frightful dilemma is created. While all love may end in the tragedy of loss, as C. S. Lewis said so well, not to love is the very definition of hell. The child who resists significant relationships (bonding) faces the same bleak choices.

Children are too often left to drift in foster care. This poses a nearly impossible dilemma for foster parents. Foster care is intended by law to be temporary. Unfortunately, in the real world, it is not. Children and their foster parents may become bonded over the time spent living together. Such relationships are often carelessly interrupted and the child suffers serious harm from the loss of family and friends.

The rights of the child are paramount, according to the 1997 Adoption and Safe Families Act. ASFA shifted the legal emphasis from the absolute right of birth parents to the child's own need and right for safety and a secure home. Bonding and permanence are legally recognized as issues critical to a child's development.

Permanence is the outward expression of bonding. Every child has the right to a permanent home. Bonding and permanence are the reverse side of one another. Bonding is psychological. Permanence is the necessary milieu or the objective reality in which bonding may take place.

Much has been written about attachment disorders and their treatment. This book is different. First, objective definitions of attachment and bonding are provided. Second, evidence-based practices are suggested to help foster parents, therapists, attorneys, and judges find a permanent home for every child.

Bonding and permanence are critical issues. Clear and evidentiary definitions for key terms are provided, along with factual data to predict outcomes. When does an attachment pass the tipping point and develop into a bond, a relationship so strong that its rupture tears a hole in the lives of the persons involved? What do the statistics show about the immediate and later-life effects in increasing the likelihood of ental illness, crime, homelessness, and poverty?

How can foster parents help? What is the role for caseworkers and psychologists?

How can the case for bonding and permanence be presented in court? Federal laws and state welfare policies are provided, together with appellate court decisions that define and decide in favor of bonding in disputed adoptions.

We, the authors, are grateful for the attorneys who have worked extensively with foster children and been our advisors as we prepared this book. Thank you, Peter Kenny and Mark Bontrager.

We thank my grandson, Patrick Kenny, for his detailed editing, and my son, Bob, for his thorough and detailed formatting.

We have nine adopted children between our two families, and have had many more foster children. We appreciate the down-to-earth experience so lacking in sterile manuscripts, sometimes teaching us more than we wanted to know. We are grateful to them all for the wisdom and common sense they forced on us. Thanks to all of you. You made us grow up.

Finally, we thank our spouses.

To Mary, my wife and lifetime partner in raising our children, for her constant wisdom and practicality, and for her careful editing of this book.

To Ken, my husband and best friend, for his constant encouragement, patience, and support as I pursue my dreams.

James Kenny and Lori Groves

Part One:
The Problem

CHAPTER ONE

BROKEN PROMISES

> *"When we send our own eighteen-year-olds out into the world, it's with the tacit understanding that they aren't really on their own. We're as close as the nearest phone, ready to provide counsel about how to cope with unexpected emergencies of the everyday variety....But rarely have we been asked to reflect on the special challenges that older youth face as they leave a system that has fed and housed them and seen to their medical and educational needs. In most states, when these children turn eighteen, social workers close their cases. The assumption is that they are ready to be independent. But once they are emancipated from the system, many seem simply to melt away into society's cracks."*
> (President Jimmy Carter, 2004)

One year is a long time in the life of a child. As one Indiana judge put it, when you are in third grade, it's a long time till lunch. Waiting is painful, especially for a child. Waiting for permanence is even more painful and damaging.

The Adoption and Safe Families Act (ASFA) was passed in 1997 to stop the delay. This law stipulates that reunification with the birth family should be pursued vigorously, but it also sets certain time limits. In cases where reunification is deemed inadvisable from the start, it need not be pursued at all. In other situations, the permanency plan can be changed from reunification to another permanency option after six months. In any case a termination of parental rights (TPR) must be filed after a child has been in foster care for 12 consecutive months or 15 of the past 22 months. At the same time, federal and state subsidies are provided to encourage adoption. Sadly, as delays, red tape, and continuances ensue, deadlines are ignored. The promise of early permanence for the waiting child is broken.

Over 783,000 children and youth, one percent of the child population, were served in the foster care system during 2007. In September, 2007 there were 496,000 currently in foster care. (Casey Family Programs, 2009)

How We Break Our Promise

Legislative and case law define foster care as temporary. In actual fact, it is not. The average time nationally spent in foster care as reported in 2006 was over two years (28 months.) The average child in foster care lived in two to five different homes over a period of 30 months. Seventy thousand children in the U. S. have languished in foster care for more than five years. If ASFA were followed, the average stay in foster care would be less than one year. What has gone wrong?

1. Foster care is intended to be temporary. ASFA, based on the child's best interests, set a maximum time of 12-15 months. Yet children still remain well beyond the safe time in temporary care. National data from AFCARS in 2006 reveals the following length of stay for children exiting foster care.

15 percent under one month
34 percent from 1 to 12 months
23 percent from 12 to 23 months
12 percent from 23 to 35 months

11 percent from 35 to 59 months
5 percent over five years

Approximately one-half million children were in foster care in 2006. Slightly less than half exited foster care within the one year maximum deadline urged by the 1997 Adoption and Safe Families Act (ASFA.) In simple terms, we failed to find approximately 260,000 children a safe and permanent home within "child safe" time.

2. Failed Reunification: Between 50 and 75 percent of children placed in out-of-home care eventually reunify. Between 20 and 40 percent of those reunified, however, re-enter foster care. Children who reunify with their birth families after placement in foster care have more negative outcomes than youth who do not reunify. (Taussig et al, 2001) The data suggests that reunification may sometimes be too hasty or ill-considered.

3. Waiting for Adoption: Of the more than 500,000 children living in foster care, 129,000 cannot return to their families and are awaiting adoption. These children spend an average of three and a half years in foster care after they have become eligible for adoption. The average overall stay for children awaiting adoption is 44 months. (www.childrensrights.org)

4. Emancipation or "Aging Out": Of the 287,000 US children who exited foster care in 2005, 17 percent were adopted and 9 percent (25,000) were "aged out" or emancipated without a permanent home. (AFCARS) Youth emancipated to independent living from foster care are more likely to become homeless, poor, mentally ill, and criminals. They are also more likely to drop out from school, become unemployed, and pregnant.

The Child's Rights Are Paramount

Children have the right to grow up whole and sane. Parents, on the other hand, have both the responsibility and the right to raise their "own" children. Where do these two sets of rights conflict? Whose rights have precedence?

"The child's health and safety shall be the paramount concern." (ASFA, Sec. 101(a)) The 1997 Adoption and Safe Families Act makes clear the primacy of the child's rights. Rights are based upon needs. We all have the right to what we need, and basic needs take precedence over more sophisticated ones. By identifying "health and safety" needs, ASFA is indicating that the child's basic needs supersede the less basic needs of the parent to raise a child.

Rights flow from basic needs. Human beings have a hierarchy of needs according to Maslow (1968), with needs for food and warmth, health and safety, taking precedence over higher level needs of belongingness, power, and self-actualization. The more basic the need, the more dominant the right. The child's needs for health and safety are related to sanity and life itself. They have priority over the parents' needs for belongingness, control, and fulfillment in caring for a child as he grows.

The Rights of the Child

The UN Convention on the Rights of the Child (1990) states early in its Preamble: "....The family, as the fundamental group of society and the natural environment for the growth and well-being of all its members and particularly children, should be afforded the necessary protection and assistance so that it can fully assume its responsibilities within the community...The child, for the full and harmonious development of his or her personality, should grow up in a

10

family environment, in an atmosphere of happiness, love, and understanding...." While most would agree with that statement, the United States has still not signed this international agreement on the rights of children. The only other country not to have signed is Somalia.

Far from a finished product, the child is going through a process which will determine what kind of adult he will become, and to what extent he will be capable of working and loving. Life pathways for the child are still being fashioned. The parents, for better or worse, have already reached a stage in life where patterns, personality, and character are set.

Basic needs for a secure attachment, health, and safety must come first and provide the foundation for growth. When society removes a child from an unsafe home, society assumes an obligation to make the situation better, to make the birth home a safe one or to find an alternate permanent placement for the child. As society's most vulnerable citizens, foster children should have a primary claim on our collective conscience.

The basic needs of the child endow him or her with certain basic rights. They are threefold: 1. The right to safe surroundings. 2. The right to maintain significant relationships. 3. The right to a permanent home.

1. The right to safe surroundings: ASFA declares that the "health and safety" of the child are paramount, and that this consideration must dominate all others. The three basic rights listed above are an attempt to define the meaning of "health and safety." The right to safe surroundings is elemental and obvious.

Kulp lists nine rights which she feels must be available to children if they are to have a chance to grow up to be loving and productive human beings. Preeminent among them is "the right to food, safety, supervision, and protection." (1993)

Children have the right to be free of abuse and neglect. The welfare department is required to investigate physical abuse, sexual abuse and neglect. Of the three, neglect may well be the most devastating and is too often ignored because it is harder to substantiate.

When the safety and health of the child are at stake, all voices must be fully heard. To protect the child, the welfare department and the courts must have full knowledge. The legal parent, the Court-Appointed Special Advocate (CASA) or Guardian Ad Litem (GAL), and the foster parent must all be fully heard. Foster parents are often given minimal say or even excluded in court.

2. The right to maintain significant relationships: Bonding is a significant attachment, not some "warm fuzzy" notion described by a well-meaning child advocate. To be given the importance it deserves, bonding needs to be well defined, and the consequences of its interruption need to be made clear. (See www.adoptioninchildtime.org.)

Too often blood relationships are given undue preference and bonding is ignored. A bonded relationship may be more important to the child than mere kinship. Welfare departments and courts need to hear both sides in permanency hearings and in disputed adoptions. Moving a child from a bonded relationship is traumatic.

What happens when bonding is disrupted? Strong statistical evidence is offered in Chapter Three and following that shows a significant increase in mental illness, crime, and homelessness. To allow delay to increase the likelihood of these serious consequences represents child abuse and neglect.

Blood relatives are important. If and when the child is removed from the home of his legal parents, relatives who are available, acceptable, and willing to care for the child should be given priority. However, to locate blood relatives after time has passed and bonding with a foster family has occurred, and then to attempt to transfer the child to unknown relatives is irresponsible, harmful, and wrong. Bonding takes precedence over "kin-come-lately."

People are the medium through which our needs are met, and people are not interchangeable. All children in care have the right to the preservation of significant relationships based on the child's needs. When a child has come to depend on a specific person to meet basic needs, that person and the needs become identical in the child's mind. To take away the person is to take away the secure feeling that basic needs will be met. While the argument might be made that the child will learn in time that others can meet those basic needs, there is risk that the child will turn his emotions off and refuse to attach again, rather than face future rejection. The DSM-IV lists frequent changes in foster care as a factor in the diagnosis of Reactive Attachment Disorder.

3. The right to a permanent home: Children need stability and permanence. A child cannot grow and develop without a firm and unchanging base. Even a less-than-best home is preferable to being shuffled around, never knowing where one belongs. Children can adjust to most situations. They cannot adjust to not knowing what happens next or not knowing where they will be tomorrow. One cannot get the momentum to spring forward from a base that moves around. In the face of uncertainty, the child can only hang on and hope for stability.

One year in a child's life is already a long time. Recognizing this as the maximum interlude allowable for impermanence, ASFA requires that a termination of parental rights be filed within that time and no later. The choice between reunification with the legal parents or adoption must be made wisely but quickly, within the one year of "child time." Delay abuses the child.

The Pain of Waiting

Waiting is painful, even torturous for adults. Ignorant of the outcome, one is likely to imagine every possibility, and especially the worst. Failing to provide a permanent home for a child is to break a promise that is implied when the child is removed. The very fact of removing a child suggests that the state will improve the situation. And yet many children suffer a painful and often fruitless wait.

The tragedy of a coal mine disaster is heartbreaking. Remember the relatives waiting on the surface for news of their loved ones? The pain of not knowing, even for those of us who were mere spectators, was very difficult to endure.

Imagine you are awaiting the results of your mammogram exam or prostate test. You call daily but they still don't have the results. What are you thinking? Feeling?

Pretend you are working as a temp, hoping to get a full-time job so you can have access to benefits and support your family. The months slip by. You are doing a good job but are afraid even to inquire whether they plan to hire you. Nothing is happening. You are worried but try not to let it show.

Waiting is much longer and much worse for a child living in a home with no permanent commitment. Most adults have other life experiences, memories of times when patience was rewarded with good results. Adults learn to hang in there on the big issues and "not to sweat the small stuff." The child has no such reassuring experiences. Imagine you are a four-year-old that has just been ripped from your birth parents by the police. Screaming and crying, clutching only a doll, you are handed from the police officer to a strange lady. This lady puts you in a car and tells you that you are going to live with a new family. Scared and alone, you don't understand what is happening. Bewildered, you arrive at strange house. You wonder why you are here. Can you play? Will they feed you?

As you go through a new routine, not knowing what is expected of you, you wonder: "Where is my mom?"

What happens to a child who has been traumatized by events much like these? The child wonders, "Am I going home?" But the question never gets answered.

Extensive psychological research has documented the negative consequences of delay. Harm results from drifting along in foster care. ASFA reflects this concern by setting deadlines for permanence. Yet too often, the state moves from abuse by the birth parents to further abuse by the welfare departments and courts, the very systems that were designed to protect the child.

The foster child's whole life and future are on the line. He will not understand all the bureaucratic reasons adults may provide to explain the delay. He is much more likely to interpret a lack of results as a lack of love. "If you loved me, you would promise to be there forever for me."Or even worse, the child may wonder whether it is his or her own fault. "Why doesn't anyone want me? I must not be lovable." So why do we fail to show the urgency that the research and laws insist upon?

Why We Break Our Promise

ASFA is a good law with a promise of a safe home within one year at most. So, why the discrepancy between law and compliance? Many reasons have been given to explain the delays.

No sense of crisis: The institutions designed to protect the children have no sense of crisis. We should treat foster care like hospitalization. When the crisis has passed, get back home – or find a new one. The longer a child is in temporary care, the more damage is done. Evidence shows significant correlations between the length of time in temporary care and increased mental and social problems. Unfortunately, caseworkers and courts do not feel this sense of urgency.

Getting it right takes time: Another reason sometimes given by caseworkers is that they must wait until they are certain that they have it right. No matter how "right" the initial case plan or the final resolution may be, a sure way to get things wrong is to delay. While the system dithers, the child is growing and developing, both physically and psychologically. The problem is that the child does not have time. The clock is ticking. The perfect becomes the enemy of the good.

The high turnover and a shortage of caseworkers: Caseworkers come and go. Foster children are transferred from one staff member to another, and left to drift, under the assumption that they are safe in the foster home. Many caseworkers are not sufficiently trained in child development.

Older children should be allowed to choose whether they want to be adopted: This is a tough one. The young person must have a voice. Yet most 14-year-olds have a naïve idea of how the world works, and what it takes to survive as an adult. They may brashly want to be free of any parental controls. They may have hopes of being reunited to an idealized birth parent, having forgotten the neglect and abuse they earlier experienced. They may be responding with rejection to the way that society has thus far treated them.

The child's rights are not given priority: Many courts and judges have still not grasped this basic concept of ASFA, which states that the child's rights are paramount. The child's right to a permanent home supersedes the rights of the birth family, the foster parents, and the prospective adoptive parents. The child's rights come before the state's need to save money. The first consideration must be what is best for the child. And yet many judges retain a lasting bias toward birth mother, giving her endless opportunities to improve, letting terminations drag on year after year.

Children are our most valuable resource, our hope for the future. Foster children are our most vulnerable citizens. Concern for their well-being must have the highest priority. Delays in establishing permanence add to an already negative situation. Every child has the right to a permanent home within a year.

"I don't think they (people) understand how it feels not to say 'mom' and 'dad'....Going through foster care, you don't get to say that, you know that often. And if you do trust somebody enough to say that, who knows how long they'll stick around." (Iowa foster youth: Quoted in Jim Casey Youth Opportunities Initiative, March, 2007)

CHAPTER TWO

WHAT EVERYONE NEEDS TO KNOW ABOUT BONDING

> *Bonding is a significant reciprocal attachment which both parties want and expect to continue and which is interrupted or terminated at increased peril to the parties involved.*

Bonding is vital to a child's development. Children need to connect in a compelling and significant way with those who care for them. The disruption of a bonded relationship does considerable damage. The presentation and proof of bonding between the child and the foster/adopt parents may be the strongest argument for keeping them together, especially in a contested adoption. The problem for attorneys and caseworkers is to define bonding and to prove in a factual and evidentiary way that bonding has taken place.

Childhood is short. From birth to maturity the child has much to learn. Most learning will be mediated through personal attachments and relationships. Attachments are vital to the development of a self-sufficient and loving adult. Bonding is a vitally important relationship.

Definitions of Terms

Why is it so important to define bonding in specific and objective terms? Two important reasons stand out. First, the negative consequences of interrupting bonded relationships can be severe. A hole, an emptiness exists, a time and space that cannot be recovered. An empty chair. A lonely time of day. An important task with a missing partner. That is when we know for sure that we have disrupted something important and significant. By then, however, it is too late. To anticipate and prevent the loss, we need to know beforehand.

Second, mental health professionals are often vague and fuzzy in trying to define bonding, giving opinion rather than data, generalizations rather than facts. As a result, case managers may not have given bonding the important consideration it requires. And courts do not get the objective and unbiased information they need to make critical decisions about a child's placement.

Bonding, when it occurs, can be more important than kinship. We have a genetic attachment with those persons who share our DNA. Yet many significant relationships are fashioned in other ways. Bonding refers to the strength of a relationship, not necessarily its biological source. Throughout life people may attach to one another in ways more significant and more powerful than those dictated by genes. A very close friend can become more important than a brother or sister. The most obvious non-genetic bond occurs in marriage where two people attach themselves to one another with a commitment that supersedes genetic connections and they expect that connection to last a lifetime.

Confusion between the concepts of attachment and bonding has muddied definitional clarity. These terms have often been used interchangeably. In fact, they are different. Bonding, as defined at the opening of this chapter, should be reserved to identify a significant attachment, one that is expected to last a lifetime and whose disruption is likely to cause serious and long-lasting trauma. A brief review will reveal the different ways these terms have been used, the overlap, and the failure to distinguish between them.

Attachment

"The word attachment can have several meanings. Even in professional discussion, it is often loosely substituted for bonding, relationships, or affection. Each of these can be considered a component of attachment, but....clarity of definition is essential." (Mooney, 2010)

Attachment theory was formulated by John Bowlby (1969) and Mary Ainsworth over 50 years ago to provide a framework for understanding human relationships. They posited that the purpose of attachments was to satisfy the child's need for protection and safety, to provide the secure base that is a paramount need of childhood. Here in their own words are their definitions:

- Attachment is "The dimension of the infant-caregiver relationship involving protection and security regulation. Within this theoretic framework, attachment is conceptualized as an intense and enduring affectional bond that the infant develops with the mother figure, a bond that is biologically rooted in the function of protection from danger." (Bowlby, 1982)
- Attachment is "An affectional tie that one person or animal forms between himself and another specific one – a tie that binds them together in space and endures over time." (Ainsworth, 1967)

21

Early relationships are critical, especially the mother-child dyad. "When a baby is born he cannot tell one person from another and indeed can hardly tell a person from a thing. Yet, by his first birthday he is likely to have become a connoisseur of people. Not only does he come quickly to distinguish familiars from strangers but amongst his familiars he chooses one or more favorites. They are greeted with delight; they are followed when they depart; and they are sought when absent. Their loss causes anxiety and distress; their recovery, relief and a sense of security. On this foundation, it seems, the rest of his emotional life is built – without this foundation there is risk for his future happiness and health." (Bowlby, 1966)

Bowlby is unequivocal about the near-permanent duration of attachment: "An attachment endures, usually for a large part of the life cycle....early attachments are not easily abandoned and they commonly persist." (1979)

Bowlby later states: "Attachment behavior is any form of behavior that results in a person attaining or maintaining proximity to some other clearly identified individual who is conceived as better able to cope with the world. It is most obvious whenever the person is frightened, or sick, and is assuaged by comforting and caregiving....For a person to know that an attachment is available and responsive gives him a strong and pervasive feeling of security, and so encourages him to value and continue the relationship.....It can be observed throughout the life cycle, especially in emergencies. Since it is seen in virtually all human beings ....it is regarded as an integral part of human nature." (Bowlby, 1988)

By adding cross-cultural data, Ainsworth expanded Bowlby's attachment theory. She gathered her data by observing children in a "Strange Situation" for 20 minutes, and then observing what happened when the children were reunited with their caregivers. She was able to differentiate three separate attachment styles: 1. Secure attachment, 2. Anxious/ambivalent insecurity, and 3. Anxious/avoidant insecurity. Cross-cultural studies convinced Ainsworth and Bowlby that children attached to caregivers for the purpose of achieving security, survival, and ultimately genetic reproduction. Bowlby and Ainsworth did not distinguish attachment from bonding; in fact they referred to attachment as "a tie or bond."

Main (1996) refers to attachment as a sub-category of bonding. "Attachment is a unique form of affectional bond; the term should not be used for affectional bonds in general." She goes on to state: "Attachment is a lifespan phenomenon. However, we have yet to understand the formation of new attachments in adulthood." Later she takes a strong position on attachment (we would say bonding) versus mere blood ties: "There is no convincing evidence that behavior genetics play a role in the organized categories of infant attachment observed in the 'strange situation.' Genetics may, however, interact with attachment in other ways...."

Researchers and authors all seem to have their own definition of attachment. Here are just a few:

- "An affectionate and emotional bond that will last a lifetime." (Klaus and Kennell, 1976)
- "An enduring social tie of a child to a specific person, such as a mother or father." (Mosher et al. 1987)
- "The trust and love that an infant feels toward the parent who meets its need." Bonding is reciprocally defined as "The loving return commitment by the parent to meet the child's needs." (Fahlberg, 1991)
- "All children, at the core of their beings, need to be attached to someone who considers them to be very special and who is committed to providing for their ongoing care." (Hughes, 1997)

23

- "The terms bonding and attachment are used to describe the intense emotional tie that develops between an infant and his or her primary caregiver over the first months and years of life." (Bush 2001, p.18)
- "An enduring and emotional connection between two people that produces a desire for continual contact as well as feelings of distress during separation." (Berger, 2001)
- "A strong emotional bond between a baby or young child and a caring adult who is part of the child's everyday life...." (Honig, 2002)
- "A reciprocal process by which an emotional connection develops between an infant and his/her primary caregiver. It influences the child's physical, neurological, cognitive, and psychological development. It becomes the basis for development of basic trust or mistrust, and shapes how a child will relate to the world, learn, and form relationships throughout life." (Moss, 2009)

No one can argue with these sentiments, but they pose real definitional problems. Attachment and bonding are used differently and interchangeably, or are too often perceived as "feel-good" concepts, and defined in objectively vague and emotional terms. This makes bonding difficult to present in court.

A History of Bonding Definitions

Human bonding refers to the development of a close interpersonal relationship between family members or friends. The term is from the 12th century Middle English word band, which refers to something that binds, ties, or restrains. In early usage, a bondsman, bondswoman, or bondservant was a feudal serf that was obligated to work for his or her lord without pay. Today a bondsman is a person who provides a bond or surety for someone.

Children form attachments to adults who regularly meet their physical and emotional needs regardless of biological relationship. Goldstein et al (1973) developed standards to identify this person, the psychological parent, the one to whom the child appears to have most firmly bonded. Goldstein and his co-authors believed that, in the child's best interests, the psychological parent should be allowed to become the primary and permanent caregiver.

"Obligations to stepparents, who fill the position of parents, and stepchildren, who fill the position of children, are higher than to more distant blood kin." (Rossi et al, 1990) Proximity and living together are a more important connection than that of distant blood relatives. Bonded relationships develop when people live together in family situations.

According to Rossi et al (1990), bonded relationships endure and last a lifetime. If, as we shall see, the interruption of a bonded relationship can cause severe damage, we need to know when that line is crossed. When does the "tipping point" from attachment to bonding occur? We do not want to wait until the life has been lived and the harm has been done.

"A bond can be defined as a unique relationship that is specific and endures through time. Although it is difficult to define this enduring relationship operationally, we have taken as indicators of this attachment various kinds of behavior between parents and infants, such as kissing, cuddling, and prolonged gazing – behavior than maintains contact...." (Klaus et al, 1995)

Goulet et al (1998) list three essential characteristics of bonding: proximity, reciprocity, and commitment. These characteristics are contained in our definitive criteria to document bonding.

25

Reciprocal Connectedness was introduced as a concept by Arredondo (2000) to expand Bowlby's one-way notion of bonding. "This neurodevelopmental concept describes a phenomenon that does not reside within the child alone but depends on an available adult who interacts reciprocally with the child....It encompasses a broader range of childhood needs, including interactive verbal and nonverbal communication, responsiveness, modeling, reciprocal facial expressiveness, social cues, motor development, and other dimensions necessary for normal neurodevelopment."

Iwaniec (2006) reviews the definition problem between bonding and attachment. She states: "Bonding is generally believed to be a bi-directional, reciprocal process. It has also been defined as a cognitive and social process that develops through positive feedback and satisfying experiences between the attachment dyad."

Bonding Defined

In order to have meaning in court, the definition of bonding needs to be clear, specific, and objective. The state Child Welfare Manuals are a good place to start for such practical definitions. The 2000 Indiana Child Welfare Manual gives three examples of situations that would warrant an exception from the rule that efforts be made to find an adoptive placement which does not require post-adoption subsidies. All three refer to bonding, indicating that the protection of a bonded relationship is in the child's best interest and more important than money. The examples are:

- The child has been in the foster home for six months or more.
- The child has already developed a significant emotional attachment to the foster parents.

- The child desires to be adopted by his foster parents.

Four concrete and evidentiary definitive criteria for bonding emerge from the current research. They are contained in one way or another in many state child welfare manuals. Any one of them standing alone is sufficient to demonstrate that bonding has occurred. The criteria are: length of time, the behavior of the child, reciprocal attachment, and family identification

Time in Place: In a parent-child family setting, bonding may take place after three months. Research from many venues indicates that three months is the length of time that normal human beings take to adjust to a new and/or difficult situation. This three-month period is reflected in folk wisdom as the time of grieving after a death, and also as the probationary period when starting a new job. In the description of many psychiatric disorders listed in the DSM-IV (1994), three months is the time allowed to "adjust" before a more serious illness can be diagnosed.

Bonding is probable after six months. Normal children will adjust and attach well within this time frame. ASFA and the parallel state laws recognize this fact by setting six months as a turning point after which a permanency plan other than reunification may be selected.

Bonding is almost certain after one year, unless one is dealing with an unbonded or psychopathic child. In such cases the child, without therapy, is not capable of bonding with anyone. Even in such cases, when bonding on the child's part is absent, the court should recognize the willingness of the foster/adopt parents to make a lifetime commitment, which is of considerable value both to the child and to society.

Time is the definitive factor. Bonding is possible after three months, probable after six, and almost certain after 12 months. At some point the child's right to permanence and emotional stability must come before the rights of the biological parents. Recognizing that a year is a very long time in the life of a developing child, ASFA requires that the state file a termination of parental rights within that time period. Continuing delay, even to grant biological parents extra chances, is destructive to the child.

Biological parents must be given immediate help and the opportunity to change neglectful or abusive behavior. But they must do so within a reasonable time. If a year goes by and the biological parents are still not ready for reunification, and the child has bonded with another family, then the child's right to a permanent stable home becomes pre-eminent. This pre-eminence exists even though the biological parents may not be at fault. Biological parents cannot be given unlimited time and chances to reform their lives.

The Behavior of the Child is a second way to determine whether bonding has occurred. Research suggests that bonding can be established by the way a child interacts. Young children who are bonded seek to stay close to the parent or caregiver. They turn to the parent when frightened, hurt or distressed. They may object when the parent leaves them. They want the parent to watch and admire what they do. (Belsky et al, 1988.)

Checklists can be used to determine and measure these behaviors clinically (Randolph, 1997; Keck, 1998.) Here are a few examples from the Groves Bonding Checklist which contains 49 such behaviors. See Appendix F for the complete list.

Eye contact
Being affectionate with "parents"
Enjoying hugs and physical contact
Attentiveness to what is going on

Copying mannerisms of "parents"
Asserting self
Going to "parents" when hurt or distressed
Being able to express pleasure and joy
Being kind to animals, and many others.

Bonding is Reciprocal. Measuring the interaction between the parent and child is a third way to measure bonding. Arredondo (2000) posits a "reciprocal connectedness" which he characterized as a mutual interrelatedness characterized by reciprocity and developmental sensitivity.

Stokes and Strothman (1996) focused on the mutual interplay in presenting their structured dyadic interview to assess the strength of the parent-child relationship.

In addition to noting the existing track record of the foster/adopt parents with the child, a good bonding assessment will include the commitment they are offering. The bonded parent is the one who wants to raise the child through good times and bad, through joy and heartbreak, until death. The evaluator may request a statement from the foster/adopt parents expressing the strength of their commitment.

"I want you to be my child forever. I will always be there for you. As long as I live. Even after you are 18 and emancipated. You won't ever be absent from my concern. Our home will always be your home. When life hits you hard and you need a place to go. When you need money. When you go through a divorce. Or a death. When I die, you will have an inheritance. You will always have a place here with me." The child's willingness to respond to and accept that promise should also be considered.

Family Identification is a fourth way to measure bonding. The Indiana Child Welfare Manual (2000) is practical and explicit in directing case managers to identify and protect bonded relationships with the foster parents by validating the cumulative wisdom of the community. Specific guidelines to prove that bonding has occurred were provided:

(1) The child identifies as a member of the foster family.
(2) The child is perceived to be a member of the foster family by the community: e.g. the   school, friends, neighbors, extended family members.
(3) The child has developed self-reliance and a trust of the foster family while in their care.
(4) The child does not make a significant attempt to attach to another family, including the birth family.
(5) To demonstrate bonding using the "family identification" criteria, the evaluator may wish to include statements from the extended family, teachers, friends, and neighbors.

Many different definitions of attachment and bonding appear in the research history. They focus mainly on the internal and emotional interaction, particularly between mother and infant. The definition of bonding proposed in this book is more external and objective, describing what bonding looks like, and what it does. Bonding needs to be framed in a way that does not depend solely on the feelings of the parties involved. Here are some key qualities that have appeared in the research.

- Bonding is a form of **attachment**.
- A **significant** attachment. The relationship is critical to both parties.
- Bonding is **reciprocal** or mutual. Both parties want the relationship.

- Bonding involves **commitment.** The quiet promise expressed in the day-to-day caregiving transcends any emotional moment.
- Bonding takes **time** to develop.
- Bonding is **natural**. It develops in everyday relationships, not in a therapy office.
- Bonding requires day-to-day **proximity**. It normally develops in a family setting.
- Bonding is or is expected to be **lifelong**.
- Bonding means **interdependence**. Both parties are attached in a vital way
- The interruption of bonding can cause serious **distress**. Childhood and adult mental disorders are the frequent result of disrupting bonded relationships.
- **Permanence** is the key structure. A permanent home is the external marker of bonding.

Permanence, as evidenced by a permanent home, is both the sign and the necessary setting for bonding. Without a secure and trustworthy base, bonding is almost impossible. A permanent home is like the dream goal, the "final frontier" in the journey of a foster child through failed reunifications, multiple placements, and temporary care.

Finally, we come to our proposed objective definitions of terms. Attachment is the general term. Bonding is the highest and most intense form of attachment. Bonding can be differentiated from attachment by the eleven qualities listed above. These qualities are expressed more succinctly in the following definition:

Bonding is a significant reciprocal attachment which both parties want and expect to continue, and which is interrupted or terminated at increased peril to the parties involved. Bonding occurs naturally over time by sharing important events in daily life such as eating sleeping, and playing together.

What Bonding Is Not

Bonding may be more clearly understood by differentiating it from what it is not.

Bonding is not everything. Bonding evaluators have sometimes adopted the "kitchen sink" approach, using a broad smorgasbord of evaluative procedures, including psych testing, mental status exams, and parenting skills. The important issue of bonding is weakened and gets lost among other important factors.

A bonding evaluation is not a custody evaluation. Bonding is very important, but still only one factor. Bonding does not suffice to determine the best placement for a child. A good custody evaluation will include information about the physical and mental health of all parties, financial matters, and the actual home setting.

Bonding is not mere attachment. Attachment refers to a variety of relationships. Bonding is one specific type of attachment. Because of its general nature, attachment admits of categories and hierarchies. People can grow in their relationships and become attached to some more than to others. Bonding goes beyond attachment and usually involves a lifetime commitment. This type of commitment is rare.

Bonding is not simply being together. Although being on the same softball team or frequenting the same bar has been referred to as "male bonding," that falls far short of our definition. "Girls' night out" is in the same category.

Bonding is not a single shared memorable moment. Sharing something profound such as being cancer survivors, the death of a child, or being with someone when something transformative happened such as 9/11 is not bonding. These shared experiences may be deep and unforgettable, but they are not so significant that their loss leaves a hole, a person that cannot be replaced, an emptiness that cannot be filled.

Bonding is not superficial. Anything but. Bonding meets vital needs at every level of development. As an infant, our very life depends on the bond with our caregiver. Throughout life, bonding provides the secure base to allow us to satisfy more sophisticated needs like self-esteem and self-actualization.

And finally, although they are often confused, **bonding is not love.**

- Love can be one-sided. Bonding is mutual.
- Love can become an obsession. Bonding is a steady need.
- Love is more emotional. Bonding is more tangible and practical.
- Love is exciting. Bonding is more "quiet" and everyday.
- Love is enhancing. Bonding is gripping.
- Love is almost always seen as emotionally positive. Bonding is neutral.

Bonding Myths

Because bonding has often been so vaguely defined, some misconceptions or myths have arisen, which sadly seem to serve the purposes of those expounding them. These myths about bonding need to be addressed and discounted.

MYTH ONE: No harm is done when an infant or small child is moved from home to home because they will not remember the experience later. False.

According to almost every expert, the initial year of life is critical in child development. The principle of primacy over recency applies. The earlier in life an event occurs, the more significant are its consequences.

The first two years of a child's life are pre-verbal. Since early life experiences are not mediated and analyzed by words, they make a more generalized and lasting impression than later ones. Erikson (1950) posits that the lifelong attitude whether to trust or distrust the world is formed in the first year or two. If an infant's mother is not there to meet basic needs, the baby's whole world falls apart. If, however, a teen feels that his mother is non-responsive, he may figure that she has had a bad day and look elsewhere.

Infants generalize. If one important person leaves, they may well perceive that they are unlovable and that the world is not to be trusted. Separation and loss are hard for an adult, but they are catastrophic for a small child.

Child development can be compared to the ocean voyage of a ship from New York to Spain. A small navigational error made just short of the Spanish port might cause the ship to scrape the dock. That same error made in the beginning while leaving New York might cause the ship to miss the entire coast of Spain. The earlier a consequential event occurs in life, the more it determines later patterns of adjustment.

MYTH TWO: The child who has bonded well in one family is a "good bonder," and will do well if moved to another family. This is totally wrong. Humans do not bond or love generically. They bond to this particular person in this particular place.

When first placed in a foster home, some children appear superficially pleasant and charming. The "honeymoon" may last as long as three months. This is the exact opposite of a healthy attachment. Entering a new placement, the pseudo-bonder exhibits the desired manners. The goal is not to form an emotional connection, but as a way to manipulate the new parents. Some psychologists and social workers have naively

34

believed that multiple placements have taught children how to bond quickly and easily. In fact, experienced foster parents have learned to be wary of the child who comes on too quickly. Bonding always takes time.

Remember what was said earlier about the marriage bond? Suppose that you have been happily married for two years when the kindly well-meaning person in charge of your life announces, "You are such a good bonder that we have decided to move you. Tonight you are going to a different home with a different husband. It is a very nice place, and he is a wonderful person. You're really going to like it there." Crazy? No more crazy than telling a bonded foster child that he will do or be well moving to a new placement.

MYTH THREE: Bonding is a skill. Both parents and children can learn the skill of becoming "good attachers." Wrong again. Learning good manners and how to get along pleasantly and superficially is a skill, but it is very different from bonding. True bonded relationships, in fact, may involve conflict and at times be stormy.

Bonding is more elemental than the skill of good manners. Bonding is what happens to normal people over time when they share meals and bedtime stories, chores and recreation, watch TV and play video games together, go shopping and to baseball games. Bonding is part of the process of living together. Bonding takes time and being together day after day.

In the past, foster parents in their training were sometimes counseled not to become too attached to the children given to their care. This counsel assumes mistakenly that bonding is something over which people have conscious control. Bonding happens to people who live together for a significant period of time. Frankly, one might question the caring commitment and emotional response of foster parents who did not become attached to the children in their home.

MYTH FOUR: Bonding can grow and develop through regular visitation. Wrong. People may become acquainted in that way but bonding is not likely to occur, only continuing frustration.

This is a common mistake made in an attempt to involve a latecomer in the permanency plan. The child may have already bonded to his or her long-term foster/adopt parents. Then a blood relative arrives late on the scene and makes known their wish to adopt. Visitation is ordered by the court to initiate a bonding process. Bonding, however, won't happen that way and may only put the child through an unnecessary and sometimes painful game of peek-a-boo. Goldstein et al (1973) make clear that the psychological parent is not someone the child visits but rather the child's primary and everyday caretaker.

A better solution than prolonged visitation to see "if it takes" would be to determine the forever parent first. If the court chooses the blood kin, then the child can be placed accordingly, and provided with a realistic opportunity for bonding to take place in the now permanent home.

Bonding can occur when people come together day after day in elemental ways and meet one another's basic needs: for food, shelter, play, friendship, and love. This may happen laterally as in a mutually actualizing marriage. Or it may happen vertically as between parent and child where the partners fulfill different but still vital needs. The parents fulfill the child's needs for food, shelter, and nurture. The child conversely fulfills the parents' need for purpose, completion, and love. Bonding will not occur over a weekend or through afternoon visitations at a welfare office or fast food restaurant.

MYTH FIVE: Kinship comes first, no matter what or when. Not true. The words relative and related obviously have the same root. Blood is one way we are related, but bonding is another. The questions should be asked: Which relationships are most critical for this child? To whom is the child most closely related psychologically? These relationships need to be examined and compared, with the child's best interests in mind.

White middle-class culture focuses narrowly on the nuclear family. Other cultures, notably our black and Hispanic communities, acknowledge the extended family network that provides physical, financial, and emotional support. The terms grandmother and grandfather, uncle and aunt, brother and sister are often applied to the persons who fill these roles. They may not be blood relatives but they are truly related in a substantive and vital and way. Questions like "Who is living in the home?" and "Who helps you out?" may help identify these bonded but non-genetic relatives.

The mistake in Myth Five is to assume that blood ties are the only ties, or that they are necessarily more vital than bonding.

How Bonding Develops

Greg Mortenson (2006) became lost on his way down a mountain he had climbed in Pakistan. Near death, he wandered into a small impoverished village where he was nursed and cared for. He has since returned to rural Pakistan in gratitude to build schools. One day the village elder interrupted Mortenson's hard-pressing American work ethic and got him to sit for tea. Mortenson quotes the elder's words in his best-selling book Three Cups of Tea. "Here we drink three cups of tea to do business; the first you are a stranger, the second you become a friend, and the third, you join our family, and for our family, we are prepared to do anything – even die." Bonding is that third cup of tea.

Bonding is a continuum, a progression from distance to intimacy. The togethering begins with a meeting where a tangible connection occurs, proceeding over time to friendship. The friendship may grow into an attachment. As that attachment becomes more secure and important, bonding may result. True bonding is relatively rare.

Romance follows the same pattern. The first attraction may be physical. Nice body. Strong square shoulders. Looking good. Contact is made. A spark or meeting of minds may take place. The couple must decide whether they want to pursue the relationship. If so, they begin exploring what they have in common. The two hang out, go for a walk, attend a movie or concert, or have a meal together. They are seeing how it works to do ordinary everyday things with each other. But they are still not letting their guard down.

As they get to know each other better, the relationship develops into an attachment. As that attachment deepens and becomes more secure, and with the amplification of lovemaking, bonding may occur. "I cannot live without this person. Now what do I do?" We speak of the marriage bond as the usual outcome of this process.

In many ways, the ontogeny of bonding parallels Maslow's hierarchy of needs. (Maslow, 1943) Self-actualization can only occur if one begins with a secure and firm base. That secure base begins with the meeting of physiological needs, such as food, sleep, and housing. As those needs are met, safety becomes important. Next, love and belongingness become connected with the person or situation that makes one feel safe. Humans attach to the person who meets their needs. As these needs are met, the need for self-esteem can be pursued and gratified. People internalize the way others see them. If and when they feel more confident and sure of themselves, they may proceed to self-actualization, fulfilling their higher needs for religion and art and beauty.

The ultimate self-actualization is inter-dependence, where we find another with a soul like our own and there is a mutual meeting of needs. When two people meet one another's needs from security to joy at sharing the finer things and moments of life, that can be called mutual-actualization. That can also be called bonding.

Sibling Bonding

What about bonding between siblings? Children bond to one another over time in the same way it happens between children and adults. Evaluating sibling relationships poses the same problem, comparing blood and bonded relationships. Being related by genes does not necessarily create a personal bond.

The bond between siblings may be the longest lasting relationship people have. When children must be removed from a birth home for cause, every effort should be made to keep the siblings together. Separating them from each other in addition to their parents amplifies the trauma. The problem is further complicated when children remain in a foster home for six months or more and bond to their foster brothers and sisters.

An effort should be made to keep siblings together initially. But what if the first pre-adoptive home is unwilling or unable to adopt additional biological siblings? What if the child to be adopted has never met or known his other siblings? What if the child, in the meantime, has formed bonds with a new set of brothers and sisters? Biological siblings and other blood relatives are sometimes discovered too late. Disrupting bonds to place heretofore unattached biological siblings together is psychologically damaging. If a child is free for adoption and the foster family has had the child for more than six months and wishes to adopt, that family usually represents the child's best option for permanence.

Who are the child's most important brothers and sisters? Are they the ones with the same biological parents? Or the ones with whom the child has been raised for a significant period of time? What if a choice must be made between a "blood" brother and the foster brother with whom the child has bonded? What about half-brothers? Step-sisters? Foster brothers? Sisters of the heart? The dictionary defines "sibling" as a brother or sister. It goes on to define brother all the way from "a child of the same parent or parents" to a "comrade or friend." Some caseworkers and judges consider only genetic siblings, despite the general consensus for a much broader interpretation.

The word "sibling" refers to a child's relationship with a peer with whom he lives and who plays a significant role in his life. Relationships between children are established in a variety of ways:

1. Through a sharing of genes.
2. Through a significant attachment known as "bonding."
3. Through friendship, an important but less vital relationship

The same definition of bonding applies to sibling relationships as it does to parent/child connections. Bonding is a significant reciprocal attachment between children which both parties want and expect to continue, and which is interrupted or terminated at considerable long-term peril to the persons involved. Bonding results from sharing over time important events in daily life, such as eating, sleeping, and playing together.

Bonding between children who live together can be evaluated according to the same four criteria used with parent and child: Time, Behavior, Reciprocity, and Family Identification. As stated earlier, bonding may occur after three months together, is probable after six, and almost certain after 12 months.

No one would oppose the policy that keeps siblings together when they are first removed from an abusive home. This is important, not just because of their genetic ties, but because they have lived together and are probably bonded to each other in ways that transcend their blood tie. Every effort must be made to find a foster home that can accept all the children.

To separate a child from his siblings at the outset, and then to do it again after he has bonded to new parents and brothers and sisters, even if well-intentioned, is misguided and cruel. Worse, to remove a child from a home where he has bonded and place him back with later-born siblings or an unknown relative whom he has never known, represents a failure to understand the true function of relationships. Genetic connections are only one way that attachments come about. Bonding, when it is demonstrated, outweighs the mere sharing of genes.

Protecting both genetic and bonded relationships need not be a contradiction. Wherever possible, siblings should be placed together at the time of removal. If, however, siblings are separated for six months or more, then the new relationships that have been formed should be evaluated before disrupting them to "honor" genetics.

Family refers to the people you live with, not simply to your family of origin. Siblings are all your brothers and sisters, not only those with whom you have a blood tie, but those with whom you have shared a family life.

Multiple Attachments or Bonds

Bonding is person-specific, but it is not exclusive. What can be done when there are conflicting attachments or bonds? Older children may be significantly attached to birth parents, and subsequently, during their stay as foster children, they become significantly attached to foster parents as well. Following the research that indicates that bonded relationships are disrupted at peril, an effort should be made to maintain contact with all parties. Where foster/adopt parents already know the birth parents, this may happen naturally. A cooperative adoption may be in the child's best interests, giving the child the advantage of a stable and permanent home while still maintaining ties with the biological parents. (See Chapter 12)

A choice of home for the child must sometimes be made between competing parents or families. When bonding can be proven, then bonding should weigh more than mere genes. If the child is already bonded by definition to more than one set of parents, then the comparative strength of the bonds should be considered. The strength might be measured by comparing the length of time spent with the parties and the future prospects for permanence contained in the commitment.

Conclusion

Bonding must be defined in a careful and factual way because, as we shall see in the next four chapters, the consequences of its interruption are severe. Permanent harm may result. Bonded relationships must be given the attention and respect they deserve.

When a child who becomes free for adoption is living with and bonded to a foster family, that family should become the family of choice for permanence. Biology and genes are important, but not so important as to put unknown kin ahead of a bonded family in the search for permanence.

CHAPTER THREE

THE HIGH PRICE OF INSTABILITY

> *"Traditional wisdom knows that we can be crushed by grief and die of a broken heart, and also that a jilted lover is apt to do things that are foolish or dangerous to himself or others. It knows too that neither love nor grief is felt for just any human being, but only for one, or a few particular and individual human beings." (Bowlby, 1979)*

Stability has two faces, bonding and permanence. Bonding is the first face. We find stability in family and friends, our relationships with others, and our significant attachments, better known as bonding. When something exciting or distressful happens, we want to share that moment with someone close. We all have a hunger for intimacy. Everyone needs someone who will always be there for them.

A permanent home is the other face of stability. In the recent economic downturn, one of the two major crises people feared was foreclosure and the loss of a home. Home base. Where we live. A comfort place. Somewhere to go to lick our wounds.

Bonding and a permanent home, they are two expressions of the same concept. Both relate to what John Bowlby meant by a stable base. Prolonged foster care and emancipation to "independent" living deprive us of both.

Holiday time highlights the absence of family for a child who has been emancipated with no place to call home. Where do I go for Thanksgiving? Or Christmas? Everyone else is

45

going home for the renewal of memories and the exchange of gifts. Families are celebrating but I will be alone.

Other young adults have a place to call home: a place to bring their laundry, to borrow money, or parental person to call for advice or support. Someone who cares that today is my birthday. Not me. I have been emancipated to independent living. Who is there for me?

The Consequences of Separation and Loss

Separation and loss are critical life events. Most adults can still recall their first broken heart and how rejected and devastated they felt. They were certain they could never love or be loved again. To some extent that first loss colors the initiation and course of future romantic relationships.

From infancy on, parents and caregivers are aware of the pain and damage that separation and loss can cause. Parents anticipate this and prepare for it in many ways. The universal game of Peek-a-Boo is a playful way of hiding the face, practicing temporary loss, and then reassuring the child by uncovering the face again. Tension is usually relieved with peals of laughter.

"Young children are upset by even brief separations. Older children are upset by longer ones. Adults are upset whenever a separation is prolonged or permanent, as in bereavement." (Bowlby, 1973)

Bowlby later warns of the danger of disrupted family relationships which can result in "the emotionally detached individual who is incapable of maintaining a stable affectional bond with anyone. People with this disability may be labeled as psychopathic and/or hysterical. They are often delinquent and suicidal." (1979)

Multiple placements lead some children to develop a "social indifference" while others express the loss in "affect

46

hunger, wanting constant attention. These reactions frequently last a lifetime." (Steinhauer, 1991) (Cahn, 1996)

In his 1994 book, "Becoming Attached," Robert Karen states that subsequent research has confirmed Bowlby's attachment theory and inspired a revolution in child psychiatry. "Bowlby's broad point about the danger of early depriving separations, not only in terms of the suffering it causes but in its disturbing impact on character formation, had been made in a powerful way."

Brian, an 11-year-old foster child said it well: "You have to keep moving, and moving, and moving, until finally someone keeps you. That kind of sucks." (Whiting and Lee, 2003)

Children who experienced many placements showed an increase in misbehavior. Even children who began without problem behavior developed problems following multiple placements. Newton et al in 2000 suggest that everything possible should be done to keep placements to an absolute minimum.

What Happens When Bonding Is Interrupted?

Bonded relationships are critical in child development. When a bonded relationship is threatened or severed, trauma results. Ainsworth (1993), Maier (1994), Keck (1995), Holmes (1996), and Hughes (1997) all discuss the dire consequences of the disruption of bonding.

"Many of the most intense of all human emotions arise during the formation, the maintenance, the disruption, and the renewal of affectional bonds. In terms of subjective experience, the formation of a bond is described as falling in love, maintaining a bond as loving someone, and losing a partner as grieving over someone. The threat of loss arouses anxiety. Actual loss causes sorrow. Both situations are likely to arouse anger. On the positive side, the unchallenged maintenance of a bond is experienced as a source of security and the renewal of a bond as a source of joy." (Bowlby, 1979)

"Neither blood ties to the child nor sex of the primary caretaker seem to be as important as the relationship this person has to the child." (Fahlberg, 1979) Later, the same author lists the many negative consequences of the lack of attachment and bonding. Children develop a "What's in it for me?" attitude and exhibit the following behaviors to keep people away: poor eye contact, withdrawal, chronic anxiety, aggressive behavior, indiscriminate affection, over-competency, lack of self-awareness, control battles, and delayed conscience development.

John Pardeck in his 1984 empirical article on "Multiple Placement of Foster Children" concludes that many foster children develop important psychological ties to their foster parents that may be as strong as those with their birth parents.

"The more continuity is disrupted, be it through multiple moves or through being left too long in limbo while wardship and future plans are being contested, the greater the risk of severe and lasting personality damage...Many juvenile court judges, lawyers, and even Children's Aid Society workers still do not fully appreciate how damaging it is for a child to be left in limbo while his case is adjourned again and again to suit the convenience of the parents or the legal system." (Steinhauer, 1991)

"Child development specialists agree that the ability to form lasting bonds with any caregiver is severely reduced if a child undergoes too many separations or lingers in impermanence too long. By allowing impermanence for abused or neglected children in our care we are causing further damage. We are damaging children's capacity to form the lasting ties that make families secure and safe." (Cahn and Johnson, 1993)

The transition from foster care to independence is difficult. Thirty-seven percent of these youths experienced one or more homeless episodes, incarcerations, victimizations, or sexual assaults. (Courtney et al, 2001)

Iwaniec's 2006 review of the research lists some of the dire consequences that follow problems with bonding: "Reduced capacity to form meaningful emotional bonds with others; development of a fragile sense of self with resultant interpersonal difficulties; tendency towards negative self-evaluation; dysfunctional cognitions; and an impaired repertoire of defenses and coping strategies."

Feeney et al (2007) examined the impact of infant adoption on later adult relationships. The authors found that attachment issues and parental bonding were more important than adoption status in predicting adult relationship outcomes.

Neurogenesis refers to the formation of new brain cells, physically embedding the newborn and growing child's experiences. Recent research with brain-imaging techniques has demonstrated that the brain continues to form in response to the environment. The newborn begins its life hard-wired by genetics. However, changes in the brain can actually be observed and measured while the child learns and grows and bonds. The brain is, in a real sense, becoming re-wired, especially in relation to early life experiences and human interaction. In other words, bonding, when it can be demonstrated, is both physical and psychological.

"The fundamental characteristics of human consciousness and identity are that they are shaped and reshaped by a brain that is continually adapting to the world around us. Whether we're reading or walking, dreaming or talking, the particular impulses and pathways of the brain's billions of neurons are storing experiences, learning and unlearning, and creating us anew in the process." (Conlan, 1999)

Arredondo et al in 2000 relates life experience to changes in brain structure: "The developing cerebral cortex is exquisitely sensitive to external experiences. In other words, early childhood experiences in interaction with the outside world will, in part, determine the child's subsequent capacities in the higher human faculties. It is the bidirectional interaction (reciprocal connectedness) with a responsive external environment that supports the development of internal brain capacity for higher mental functions such as interpersonal sensitivity, empathy, compassion, and resilience."

McEwen in his 2007 chapter "Stress and the Brain," underlines the critical importance of the environment: "Early life experiences perhaps carry an even greater weight in terms of how an individual reacts to new situations. Early life physical and sexual abuse carries with it a life-long burden of behavioral and pathophysiological problems. Moreover, cold and uncaring families produce long-lasting emotional problems in children. Some of these effects are seen on brain structure and function and in the risk for later depression and post-traumatic stress disorder." The same might well be said about the interruption of bonded relationships.

The American Academy of Pediatrics issued a report in 2000 on "Early Childhood, Adoption, and Dependent Care." They note: "During the first 3 to 4 years of life, the anatomic brain structures that govern personality traits, learning processes, and coping with stress and emotions are established, strengthened, and made permanent.....The nerve connections and neurotransmitter networks that are forming during these critical years are influenced by negative environmental conditions....It is known that emotional and cognitive disruptions in the early lives of children have the potential to impair brain development.... In terms of evolution, the cerebral cortex is the part of the brain that was last to appear and the part that is most quintessentially human. In addition to language and speech (e.g., reading, comprehension, writing), it is home to mathematical abilities. More important to decision makers such as judges, however, is the fact that the cortex is the home of conscience, abstract reasoning, empathy, compassion, moral development, and social skills."

By interrupting the child with traumatic moves and separations, any attempt to bond is disrupted. The child's developing brain is severely impaired, setting the stage for learning disorders, behavioral problems, and mental or emotional dysfunction.

The Pediatric Academy issued another report in 2008 on "Understanding the Behavioral and Emotional Consequences of Child Abuse." Again, they warn of the serious consequences resulting from disruption and trauma in early childhood. "Once thought of as an enigmatic 'black box,' the brain is now seen as a complex of specialized, interactive organs, constantly developing through interaction with the environment and each other. Nowhere is this development more dramatic than in the first 3 years of life as the young brain undergoes sweeping structural change as it senses and adapts to the environment in which it finds itself."

A child who is well-adjusted in the beginning may give up after facing too many crises. Why bother adjusting? It becomes too painful to attach if one must face the crisis of loss again and again. Still more tragic, an unfortunate pattern of anticipating rejection may develop, an expectation which shapes future relationships even when the fear of loss may appear no longer realistic to an outside party..

Poet and foster child, Jaiya John, in his 2007 book "Reflection Pond," expresses the pain well: "Each successive

51

separation (trauma) leaves behind incremental wounds that blockade the avenues of a child's ability to receive and offer love just as plaque obstructs blood from flowing through arteries. Obstructed arteries bring us heart attack and stroke. Obstructed attachment channels (cognitive, behavioral, affective, spiritual, creative) bring her systemic breakdowns. These breakdowns manifest as injuries to her whole, creating further inflammation to her internal channels."

Interrupting or severing bonded relationships takes a heavy toll on human health and well-being. It is as serious as brain surgery, death or divorce. The younger the child and the deeper the bond, the more devastating is the consequence.

The trauma begins with the initial abuse and/or neglect, when a decision is made to change homes for the basic safety and good of the child. The child often sees the removal as his fault. If I were a good and desirable person, this would not have happened. When separation occurs, self-blame by the child is very common.

The foster care system is set up to provide temporary relief for the abused and neglected child while a more permanent plan is arranged. However, because of inefficiency and bureaucracy in the child welfare system and delays in the courts, the very systems designed to protect the child become major abusers. Delay, by allowing bonding to take place in the foster home, and then interrupting it again, can cause serious and lasting damage to a child. The impersonal systems create the unbonded child, the child who suffers from a failure to attach.

Unresolved separation and loss, multiple placements, long delays in limbo (over three months), and interrupted bonding can lead to psychopathy, aggression, a loss of capacity for intimacy, and mental illness in adolescence and adulthood.

Why Children Are Moved

Moving a child from one home to another is an intervention that has serious consequences and should be done only for the most serious reasons. Ideally, every move should be made as if that move were to be the last one necessary. As has been seen, the interruption of relationships in a developing child can have both immediate and long-term detrimental consequences. If this is so, why are children ever moved?

A move may be mandated by concern for the health and safety of the child. Children must be moved when their life and health, both physical and mental, are in danger. Too often, however, children are moved for less compelling reasons, when the cost to the child from moving far outweighs any benefit that might be obtained.

Unfortunately, some child welfare workers do not recognize the importance of maintaining significant attachments, nor the harm done when children are moved from home to home. Children are sometimes moved for trivial reasons, even upon whim or to demonstrate power. A compilation of complaints by foster parents from a Midwestern state revealed the following reasons why children are moved: (Kenny, 1997, unpublished)

- Because the child ran away.
- To reunite the child with other half-siblings.
- To make room for a larger sibling group.
- To place the child in a home of the same race.
- To be on the "safe side," protecting the foster child following uninvestigated and unsubstantiated charges of abuse by the parents or foster parents.
- To keep foster parents from becoming too attached.

- To accommodate birth parents who complained about the distance they had to travel to see their child.
- To punish foster parents who have made too many demands and are considered troublemakers.
- Because of a lack of communication between caseworkers and foster parents.

Emancipation to Independent Living

Mike was in seven foster homes before being emancipated. Like all foster children, he had been taught the required skills for independent living: how to find a job, rent an apartment, and balance his checkbook, cook, and so on. He was happy to say goodbye to his final foster home the day after his 18th birthday, but he left with no place to go. Mike lived in the park for two weeks, and then went to live with his aunt. She helped him find a job. He left again when she was arrested. He lost his job and went back to live in the park. By coincidence, he met up with his second foster family and they took him in. They helped him find another job and a new apartment. Unable to pay the rent on his minimum wage job, he was evicted. Then he lost his job due to erratic attendance. Once again he was adrift and alone in the world.

Mike had a high school diploma with no real job history, with no place to live, and with no family. He tried to get himself arrested at one point so he could get a good meal. By the time he was 24; he had spent all but 18 months dumpster-diving and living in the park and in shelters when there was an empty bed. (Groves et al, 2009)

AFCARS reported that 287,000 US children exited foster care in 2005. Of these children, over 25,000 (9 percent) were "aged out" or emancipated without a permanent home. Youth emancipated to independent living from foster care have suffered through the trauma of transience only to be turned loose and alone in an unforgiving world. Their problems are compounded by the lack of a supportive family. Emancipation to independent living is a fancy phrase to cover up failure in the foster care system.

"For many, leaving foster care is like going over a cliff. The general population does not give it a thought, but emancipated foster children need everything that a parent would give a child of the same age." (California League of Women Voters, 1998)

Westat reported in 1991 on the outcomes for foster children from 2 ½ to four years after their discharge from foster care at age 18:

- 54 percent of the population studied had completed high school.
- 49 percent were employed.
- 18 percent maintained a job for at least one year.
- 40 percent were a cost to the community in some way.
- 60 percent of the young women were already mothers.
- 25 percent had been homeless for a time, and their median weekly salary was $205.
- Only 17 percent were completely self-supporting.

Nightline reported in 2002 on foster care graduates, labeled the statistics as "staggering." They noted; "Of the 20,000 who age out of the foster care system each year, 40 percent fail to graduate from high school and 40 percent end up on welfare. Within two years, a third have children (mostly out of wedlock). As sobering as those numbers are, it's not until you spend time with kids just emancipated from the foster care system that you really begin to appreciate that world."

POVERTY: According to Rohter in 1992, adults with a history of foster care are significantly more likely to be below the poverty level. Adult poverty is correlated to "children living in legal limbo," that is a background in foster care. In 1994 Aldgate found that out-of-home public care is a major precursor of adult poverty.

Emancipated foster youth were found to earn an average of $6000 per year, well below the national poverty level. Emancipated females were four times more likely than their age-mates to receive public assistance. (www.heysf.org and www.childrensrights.org).

UNEMPLOYMENT: Foster care alumni experience problematic employment and financial situations. Less than half of former foster children are employed 2 ½ to 5 years after leaving foster care. Only 18 percent have maintained employment for at least one year. (www.heysf.org)

PREGNANCY: Females emancipated from foster care are four times more likely than their counterparts to become single parents prematurely. According to a midwest study, nearly half of the emancipated foster women had been pregnant at least once by the age of 19, compared to only 20 percent of their peers. (Casey, 2005).

EDUCATION: Casey in 2007 quotes national statistics in reporting that youth in foster care are less likely to graduate from high school. (www.heysf.org).
- Only 46% of former foster youth complete high school as compared to the 84% of the general population.
- Two-thirds of foster children had been suspended at least once compared to 28 percent of the general population.

- Seventeen percent had been expelled compared to five percent of the general population. (Courtney et al, 2004, p.42)
- Of the youth who have aged out of foster care and are over the age of 25, less than three percent have earned a college degree compared with 28 percent of the general population. (Casey, 2007).

"Aging out" without a permanent home increases the likelihood of a negative outcome. The problems are severe enough for a child who has been left to drift in temporary care and shifted from home to home. They are made considerably worse after age 18 when there is no fallback home or family. Not only does the child lack a forever mentor or family but the child has understandable problems in forming relationships. Facing the world with no family and lacking personal skills to fashion a new one, no wonder the young adult will become the problem for society that he is for himself.

Few of us are able to live alone for long, especially not beginners. Statistics will show that adult living skills are far from enough. Classes in independent living may provide the tools. Without the necessary basic structure however, this becomes frills without grounding, or the busywork of living without a permanent home.

Statements of Fact

- Interrupted bonding is significantly correlated with childhood and adult mental illness, with adult crime and violence, and with homelessness and poverty.
- The inability to cope with separation and loss in a growing child may set the stage for anxiety and depressive disorders and even adult psychoses.

57

- Multi-placed children are psychopaths-in-the-making. The separation from early attachments breeds anger which erupts in adult crime and violence at a significantly higher rate than within the general population.
- Homelessness is a lifestyle learned in foster care. Children who grow up without a permanent home take to the streets as adults in disproportionately large numbers, living without a family and without a roof.
- Children who are emancipated without a permanent home begin their lives with no source of family financial backing, no possibility of any inheritance, and the likelihood of beginning and ending their job careers at minimum wage. Emancipation is the final verdict on the failed pursuit of a permanent home.

Frequently at foster parent gatherings, the organizers will trot out a young man or woman who grew up in foster care and is now educated and successful in a productive career. Like Jackie Robinson dealing with racial prejudice, this poster child has beaten the odds. The fact that he is introduced at all indicates that this is an unusual person. And to become this unusual person required extraordinary talent, tremendous drive, and a good amount of luck. Rarely do all these factors come together in one person. For most in similar situations, whether young black baseball players in the 1940s or foster children at any time, the cards are so completely stacked against them that their best effort will not bring them success, but only setbacks and discouragement.

As will be seen in the next three chapters, foster children who "age out" of the system become mentally ill, spend time in jail, and are homeless at disproportionate rates.

PART TWO:
THE HARM DONE BY FAILURE
TO PROVIDE PERMANENCE

DELAY, DESPAIR, AND DETACHMENT
THE PHYSICAL AND MENTAL HEALTH OF FOSTER CHILDREN

Reactive Attachment Disorder: "Markedly disturbed and developmentally inappropriate social relatedness in most contexts, beginning before age five years, as evidenced by either (1) or (2):

(1) persistent failure to initiate or respond in a developmentally appropriate fashion to most social interactions. As manifest by excessively inhibited, hypervigilant, or highly ambivalent and contradictory responses (e.g. the child may respond to caregivers with a mixture of approach, avoidance, and resistance to comforting or may exhibit frozen watchfulness.)

(2) diffuse attachments as manifest by indiscriminate sociability with marked inability to exhibit appropriate selective attachments (e.g. excessive familiarity with relative strangers or lack of selectivity in choice of attachment figures.)" (DSM-IV)

T he DSM-IV indicates that Reactive Attachment Disorder (RAD) may arises from the "repeated changes of primary caregiver that prevent formation of stable attachments (e.g. frequent change in foster care.)" Interestingly, RAD is the only relational diagnosis in the DSM-IV. All the other psychiatric diagnoses involve a single person: the patient.

From Delay to Despair

Being parked in a foster home for an indefinite period is not safe. Waiting can cause serious psychological damage. Foster children in limbo pass through five emotional stages as they wait for society to find them permanence.

1. HOPE. At first the child has hope. Maybe this family will be the one. If only.... But in time, hope hurts.

2. FEAR. As hope fades, fear sets in. What if it will always be like this? What if no one really wants me? What if I never have a home? What if....

3. ANGER. After fear comes anger. The child gets mad and often expresses his feelings by acting out; temper tantrums, foot-dragging, stealing, destroying property, and failing "deliberately" in school to frustrate the foster parents.

4. DEPRESSION. The anger may fade into darkness. The child becomes quiet and sad.

5. INDIFFERENCE. In time, the depression may be replaced by a coldness, a lack of caring. So what! What's the use? Who cares? I don't.

Childhood Mental Illness

Intermittent placement and non-attachment can result in mental illness. The trauma begins when a young child is removed from a situation of abuse or neglect. Frightened, bewildered, upset, he comes to a new and totally unknown home. In time he becomes accustomed to the home, grows to like it, and attaches to the people in the home. Suddenly his caseworker comes and moves him to another home. These people are also kind to him. He likes his room, he likes the food. But he is cautious about growing attached to them. Sure enough, six months later, he moves to yet a third foster home. This time he may greet the new people warmly and smile at the right time; he may get used to the food and the bed and the new school. But he no longer feels any attachment to the family. On the outside he wears the mask of compliance. On the inside he remains apart and alone. He has learned how painful broken attachments are, and he will no longer expose himself to that kind of pain.

"Two psychiatric syndromes and two sorts of associated symptoms are consistently found to be preceded by a high incidence of disrupted affectional bonds during childhood. The syndromes are psychopathic (or sociopathic) personality and depression; the symptoms (lead to) delinquency and suicide.....The psychopath (or sociopath) is a person who, whilst not being psychotic or mentally subnormal, persistently engages in: (1) acts against society, e.g. crime; (2) acts against the family, e.g. neglect, cruelty, promiscuity, or perversion; (3) acts against himself, e.g. addiction, suicide, or attempted suicide, repeatedly abandoning his job." (Bowlby, 1979)

Bowlby writes further of the short-term effect of disrupted bonds: "In the separated children, two forms of disturbance of affectional behavior were seen, neither of which was observed in the comparison group of non-separated children.   One form is that of emotional detachment; the other its apparent opposite, namely an unrelenting demand to be close to mother." (1979)

Kulp summarizes the common pathologies of foster children that are worsened by a continuing lack of permanence. (1993)

- Delayed development in personal hygiene.
- Immaturity and poor social skills.
- Problems with authority figures (feelings of powerlessness, acting out, etc.)
- Stress reactions (fire setting, animal abuse, etc.)
- Self-destructive behaviors (lying, stealing, running away, suicide attempts, etc.)
- Difficulty in relating to others (passivity, dissociation, etc.)
- Attachment and separation problems
- Psychosomatic complaints (nightmares, stomach aches, etc.)
- Physical and mental impairments

Others followed, documenting similar lists of childhood mental disorders resulting from multiple moves.   (Karen, 1994), (Main, 1996), (Clark et al, 1998)

"Neglect, abuse, and/or multiple moves set the stage for a reactive attachment disorder resulting in children who resist relationships. These children develop pseudo-relationships with others that on the surface appear engaging, but in actuality are highly manipulative and self-serving, lacking the warmth and empathy necessary to sustain any true bonding....Examples of attachment-disordered behaviors that do not allow reciprocity include manipulation, promiscuity, instigating conflict, and theft." (Steinhauer, 1998)

Attachment problems may be an important factor that increases risk for a number of forms of childhood psychopathology. (Greenberg, 1999)

The American Psychiatric Association identifies foster care drift as one cause of "Reactive Attachment Disorder" (RAD.) If we remove a child from the biological home to protect him from abuse or neglect, then subject him to a series of foster care placements, we may have corrected the initial problem while creating another.

The American Academy of Pediatrics authorized a Committee on Early Childhood, Adoption, and Dependent Care. In their 2000 report, they stated: "The following important concepts should guide pediatricians' activities as they advocate for the child:

1. Biologic parenthood does not necessarily confer the desire or ability to care for a child adequately.

2. Supportive nurturing by primary caregivers is crucial to early brain growth and to the physical, emotional, and developmental needs of children.

3. Children need continuity, consistency, and predictability from their caregiver. Multiple placements are injurious.

4. Attachment, sense of time and developmental level of the child are key factors in their adjustment to environmental and internal stresses."

Interrupted bonding frequently leads to other psychiatric ailments in children. Included in the list of common childhood diagnoses caused by moving youngsters around are:

- Separation Anxiety Disorder
- Adjustment Disorders
- Attention-Deficit/Hyperactivity Disorder (AD/HD)
- Oppositional Defiant Disorder
- Developmental Delay
- Learning Disorder. (DSM-IV)

Separation Anxiety Disorder (SAD) is characterized by inappropriate and excessive anxiety concerning separation from home or from those to whom the individual is attached. SAD may appear as a fear of getting lost or kidnapped, a fear that attachment figures may suffer harm, refusal to attend school, a fear of being alone, sleep problems, nightmares, and repeated complaints of physical symptoms. (DSM-IV)

Adjustment Disorders are described as expressing "clinically significant emotional or behavioral symptoms in response to an identifiable psychosocial stressor or stressors." (DSM-IV) The symptoms may include depression, anxiety, flattened emotions, and/or misbehavior. The obvious stressor in foster care drift and delay is the separation of the child from a situation where he felt safe and loved.

AD/HD is described as "a persistent pattern of inattention and/or hyperactivity-impulsivity that is more frequent and severe than is typically observed in individuals at a comparable level of development." (DSM-IV) In a child who suffers the loss of a significant relationship, the failure to focus attention may be a spin-off of nonattachment. The hyperactivity, often expressed in misconduct, may be the result of anxiety and pervasive anger generated by separation.

66

Oppositional Defiant Disorder is described as "a recurrent pattern of negativistic, defiant, disobedient, and hostile behavior toward authority figures that persists for at least six months." (DSM-IV) Included among the many symptoms are loss of temper, arguing, refusing to comply, annoying others deliberately, blaming others, and being angry and vindictive. It is not difficult to surmise that being separated from a secure base may be a causative factor in the development of such strong resentment.

Being moved and shuffled around can cause a delay in development. Experts have speculated that foster children are often one to two years behind academically and emotionally. Developmental delay can appear in a variety of areas. (DSM-IV) Although developmental delay is more often due primarily to genetic and physical causes, it may also be the result of a separated child who simply decides it is easier to give up and not try.

Learning Disorders are diagnosed "when the individual's achievement on individually administered standardized tests in reading, mathematics, or written expression is substantially below that expected for age, schooling, and level of intelligence. The learning problems significantly interfere with academic achievement or activities of daily living." (DSM-IV) As with developmental delay, learning disorders may develop as the result of being shifted from home to home, from school to school.

Adult Mental Illness

Disorders of childhood generated by delays and multiple moves are mild compared to what is yet to come. The breaking of bonded relationships causes even more serious problems in adulthood. The mental disorder may surface immediately or remain suppressed for years. Pay me now or pay me later. Foster care drift may eventually create a person who lacks the ability to attach to others. While there are many contributing and confounding antecedents of adult disorders, nevertheless, adult mental illness, crime, poverty and homelessness have all been positively correlated with time spent in foster care. Problems submerged in childhood behind a veneer of compliance are apt to surface in adult life.

Childhood experiences have lifelong consequences. Foster care, even when necessary and optimal, carries with it uncertainty and the impact of rejection. Feelings of insecurity and low self-worth are a natural consequence.. The person who carries this condition into adulthood is much more vulnerable to mental, emotional and behavioral disorders.

What is mental illness? In simple terms, mental illness is a disorder of thought or behavior which significantly interferes with functioning in a major life area such as home, work or leisure time. Both the research and common sense tell us that interrupted relationships lead to withdrawal and a fear of investing in new relationships. Withdrawal and the failure to relate are at the basis of many mental disorders, including depression, anxiety disorders, and thought disorders like paranoia and schizophrenia. Even among "normal" adults, failure to form healthy emotional attachments makes stable and joyful adult family life difficult if not impossible.

"Those who suffer from psychiatric disturbances, whether psychoneurotic, sociopathic, or psychotic, always show impairment of the capacity for affectional bonding, an impairment that is often both severe and long lasting...Antecedent conditions of significantly high incidence [of mental disorders] are either an absence of opportunity to

68

make affectional bonds or else long and perhaps repeated disruptions of bonds once made." (Bowlby, 1979) The author goes on to cite a number of other studies that show a strong correlation between disrupted bonding and a significant increase in antisocial behavior, illegitimacy, and suicide.

Many researchers have written of the correlation between attachment problems among children who graduate from foster care and adult mental illness. The loss of a bonded relationship is an antecedent of multiple mental disorders. When attachments are damaged or broken, the research confirms an increase in Depression, Anxiety Disorders, Eating Disorders, Substance Abuse, Schizophrenia, Borderline Personality Disorders, and Antisocial Personality. (Triseliotis, 1993), (Aldgate, 1994), (Dozier et al, 1999)

Emancipation to independent adult living without a permanent home is the final insult. These children begin their journey by being removed from a neglectful or abusive home. They are then too often shifted from one temporary home to another and left to drift too long in foster care. Emancipating foster children to adult status without a permanent home is the final blow in a cruel and thoughtless process. According to the Casey Young Adult Survey from 2005, emancipated foster children were 2.8 times more likely to have psychotic problems, 2.5 times more likely to suffer from paranoia, 2.4 times more likely to have obsessive and/or compulsive symptoms, and 2.1 times more likely to be clinically depressed than the general U.S. population. Another study found that former foster youth were twice as likely as U.S. military veterans to suffer from post-traumatic stress disorder. (www.heysf.org)

The psychological trauma incurred through child abuse and in foster care can have serious consequences that begin in

CHAPTER FIVE

STRIKING BACK IN ANGER
DELINQUENCY AND CRIME IN FOSTER CHILDREN

Foster children are family temps
Shuffled and shunted from home to home
Often lost in time till graduation
into independent living
Their affect flattened and neutered
by society's unconcern
No surprise that they strike back
in dispassionate anger
Offending a society
that has not befriended them

Foster children are destined to grow up in uncertainty. The lack of a permanent home and foster care drift are obviously frustrating to a developing child who must find his or her elemental identity without roots and stability. To know who one is and to have the courage to venture out on one's own requires a stable base.

Detachment and the destruction of the capacity for intimacy are not the only results of long stays in foster care.

Frustration can lead to aggression. An unstable childhood generates a deep-seated and often subconscious anger. While childhood anger can be addressed and socialized in a proper setting, left untreated, it may erupt in later years.

Adult crime and violence are likely outcomes in those individuals whose empathy is stunted and who grow up without the conscience normally fashioned through a concern for the well-being of others. Add resentment and anger to a lack of compassion and you have a dangerous person in process. The psychiatric literature labels these people "psychopaths." Multi-placed children are referred to as "psychopaths in the making."

The abuse/neglect that led to removal from the birth parent home can provide the basic impetus for delinquency and adult crime. Nevertheless, delay and multiple moves may well amplify the initial anger.

Persons with a history of foster care are diagnosed at a significantly higher rate than the general population with Oppositional Defiant Disorder (ODD), Conduct Disorder, and Antisocial Personality. These DSM-IV psychiatric diagnoses are often externally expressed in delinquency and crime.

"The most violently angry and dysfunctional responses of all, it seems probable, are elicited in children and adolescents who not only experience repeated separations but are constantly subjected to the threat of abandonment." (Bowlby, 1973)

Travis Hirschi introduced his theory of Social Bonding in his 1969 book "Causes of Delinquency." His major focus was to contribute to an understanding of the causes of juvenile delinquency. For Hirschi, the 'bond' resides in the child and involves four factors or systems: Attachment, Commitment, Involvement, and Belief. Children lacking adequate levels of attachment are believed to be free from moral restraints. They are apt to act on impulse, without a conscience or feeling for others. In 2009 Kingsley reported on the considerable research done to support the Hirschi theory that the lack of relationships and attachments is a significant cause of juvenile delinquency.

The importance of social bonds in preventing delinquency is supported by many other studies:

- Over 70 percent of all State Penitentiary inmates have spent time in the foster care system. (California State Legislature)
- A federal study of former foster care wards reported that 75 percent of Connecticut youths in the state's juvenile justice system were once in foster care. (Bayles et al, 1995)
- When children are tempted to engage in unacceptable behaviors, children with strong social bonds have a greater likelihood of conforming, and are less likely to become delinquent. (Furstenberg et al, 1995)
- Eighty percent of prisoners in Illinois spent time in foster care, according to a survey by the National Association of Social Workers. (Azar, 1995)
- Problems with early attachment are seen to globalize during the adolescent years and set the stage for a failure to bond as an adult. The result is a higher incidence of both aggression and passionless crime. Greenberg in 1999 summarized the research on the links between attachment, adolescent delinquency, and adult criminality.
- A variety of studies reported that 30 to 40 percent of foster children have been arrested since they exited foster care. Over one-fourth have spent at least one night in jail and over 15 percent had been convicted of a crime. This compares with only 3.2 percent of the general population who were on probation, in jail, or on parole in 2005. (Barth, 1990) (Alexander & Huberty, 1993) (Courtney et al, 2001) (U.S. Department of Justice, 2005).

- Eighteen percent of the 20,000 children who "age out" of the foster care system each year go to jail. (Nightline, 2002)
- Almost 20 percent of young prison inmates spent part of their youth in foster care. Data further shows that 44 percent of children placed in foster care are arrested at least once, while the same was true of only 14 percent of children who stayed with their biological families. Bonding provides one interpretation of this surprising but significant difference. Children who remain in an abusive home may still have the advantage of a bonded relationship. Children in foster care are in temporary homes, subject to sudden and multiple moves, with a lack of significant attachments. (Doyle, 2007)
- Many other authors have researched and confirmed the fact that a foster care background is significantly correlated to adult crime and violence. They include Fanshel et al (1989), Steinhauer (1991), Keck (1995), Lloyd (1998), Desai et al (2000), Haapasalo (2000), and Freedman et al (2000). The evidence is overwhelming.
- Children aging out of the foster care system experience numerous difficulties, including involvement with juvenile justice and adult corrections. They are at increased risk of engaging in delinquency and crime. Residence in group homes doubled the risk for delinquency. In 2007 Ryan et al identified two major predictors of a more favorable outcome. One was school enrollment. The other was "placement stability," otherwise known as a permanent home.

The accumulating body of evidence in the above studies shows that placement instability is associated with weak attachments and juvenile delinquency. In conclusions to their own 2008 study, Ryan et al report: "Children predicting a change in placement (perceived instability) were significantly more likely to experience delinquency petitions as compared with those predicting no change in foster placement....The children that experience multiple movements within the foster care system are more likely to engage in delinquency as compared to children with no movements."

The temporary nature of foster care and its uncertainty contributes to a significantly higher outcome of delinquency and crime.

CHAPTER SIX

NO PLACE TO CALL HOME
MOVING TOWARD HOMELESSNESS

> *"A review of the literature available on homelessness reveals surprisingly more than expected on the link between out-of–home placements during childhood and homelessness. ....Findings from these studies, conducted throughout the United States, support the premise that out-of-home placements during childhood are a significant contributing factor to homelessness." (Roman and Wolfe, 1995)*

Foster Care Runaways

Running away from a foster care placement expresses homelessness as a deliberate choice. The foster youth apparently prefers the "freedom" of homelessness to imposed temporary care and systemic transience. According to a nationwide study of runaway youths, more than one-third had been in foster care before they took to the streets. (www.liftingtheveil.org)

The Congressional Research Service in 2007 reported that at the close of fiscal year 2005, close to 11,000 foster youth had run away from their placement, and that 24,000 youth "age out" of foster care each year without "proper supports to successfully transition to adulthood."

Homelessness

The authors of this book have had many older foster children. Most came to their home with a grocery sack of their few belongings. Even after years in state care, all that they owned could be carried in a bag. Better than any other term or condition, "homeless" describes the state of a child in foster care. By definition the foster child is a transient, without a permanent home.

Children who are emancipated into legal adulthood without a permanent home have no safety net, and no fallback family of origin. If they have been in foster care for an extended time, temporary living and the lack of a true home is a state they have learned while growing up. Small wonder then that foster care is correlated with homelessness. Research shows that children in foster care have a significantly high chance of becoming homeless adults.

"All sources of data support the primary finding that people with a foster care history are over-represented in the homeless population." (Roman et al, 1995) Three in ten of the nation's homeless adults report a foster care history. Child placement in foster care also correlates with a substantial increase in the length of a person's homeless experience. Their report adds that homeless parents who report a history of foster care are almost twice as likely to have their own children placed in foster care as homeless parents with no foster care background.

In a front page story, the Sunday New York Times (1991) reported that "A large and disproportionate number of the nation's homeless are young people who have come out of foster care programs without the money, skills, or family support to make it on their own." This finding was preceded and documented by a 1984 report from the Citizens' Committee for Children of New York and studies by Schaffer et al (1984), Mangine et al (1990), and a 1991 report by the National Association of Social Workers.

Adult homelessness has its roots in childhood impermanence. Extended foster care with its built-in impermanence and multiple moves represents a major risk. Little has changed over the years. The following researchers all report large numbers of homeless adults with a history of foster care: Susser et al (1991), O'Brien (1993), Blankertz et al (1993), Piliavin et al (1993), Calsyn et al (1994), Rosenbeck et al (1994), Koegel et al (1995), Herman et al (1997), Bassuk et al (1997), Zlotnick et al (1998), Cauce et al (1998), and Sumerlin et al (1999).

Roman and Wolfe (1997) in The Relationship Between Foster Care and Homelessness summarize: "There is indeed an over-representation of people with a foster care history in the homeless population...Physical and mental health problems also interact in the homelessness-and-foster-care equation...It is clear from this study that what happens to children has a lifelong impact on them. When you see homeless adults, it is quite possible that they are homeless because of people and systems that failed them as children...If it is necessary for children to enter the foster care system, extraordinary measures should be taken to move them as quickly as possible into a permanent living situation (family reunification or adoption), taking all steps necessary to avoid multiple placements."

A two-year follow up of 265 adolescents in foster care in a large urban setting revealed that 43 percent had problems finding a stable residence and 20 percent were chronically homeless. (Fowler et al, 2009)

In summary, 65 percent of emancipated foster youth leave the system with no place to go. Fifty percent will become homeless within the first 18 months. Twenty-seven percent of the homeless populations were former foster children. Fifty-eight percent of all young adults using federally funded youth shelters in 1997 had previously been in foster care. These stats are shocking but should not surprise us. By definition a foster child is a transient without a permanent home. (www.childrensrights.org)

So what can we do? The Adoption and Safe Families Act wisely allots one year as the maximum time in which to find a permanent home for children in out-of-home care. Society's challenge is to follow that mandate.

CHAPTER SEVEN

THE CHALLENGE

"Never doubt that a small group of thoughtful, committed people can change the world. Indeed, it is the only thing that ever has." (Maraaret Mead)

The Systems Are Failing

The systems designed to serve our foster children are failing. We remove children from neglectful and abusive homes with the best of intentions. The systems designed to protect and advance these children once they are in public care, however, have performed poorly. Data on outcomes which suggests how badly we have served these children have been presented in Chapter Three. The systems need to be changed. That is the challenge.

Welfare departments are surprised when foster parents want or demand a say about the children in their care. Foster parents are baffled when welfare departments oppose giving them any voice. The problem lies in their differing views of parenting.

Many welfare departments and agencies view foster care homes as boarding houses or hotels, as a place where children simply are provided with food, clothing, and shelter. Emotions are not involved. To many child welfare workers, it seems as unnecessary and troublesome for foster parents to have a say about the children as for a hotel manager to concern himself with the lives of his residents. For many welfare workers and child care agencies, bonding simply does not happen in a foster home. If it does occur, it is ignored. This may explain why some caseworkers seem to have minimal concern about moving children from home to home.

Professionals may contribute to this view when they approach bonding as a skill that can be learned in a therapist's office. They may believe that children can easily learn to adjust to loss and adapt to new situations. The truth is otherwise. Bonding is not a skill. It is a deep-seated empathic response. Interrupting bonded relationships, as noted in Chapter Three, can cause irremediable harm.

Foster parents are the only ones with everyday knowledge of the children in their care. If they have had the child on a daily basis for three months or more, bonding may have occurred. Foster parents should have a significant voice at case conferences and in court. They do not.

Change never comes easily. A failure to understand the importance of bonding in the lives of children is at the heart of our inaction. Our ignorance breeds complacency. How many times has a caseworker said: "She will be all right. She is in a good foster home." Hopefully, some of the stories and data in this book will cause enough discomfort to inform and motivate those in control. A change in knowledge and attitude must precede a change in the way people do things. Considerable pressure must be applied to overcome inertia.

Creating a sense of urgency is the first step. Change takes time; time which growing and developing children do not have. Childhood is a relatively brief period to prepare for adult life. The clock is ticking while children linger in foster care, waiting for those in charge to follow the mandated guidelines.

Reasons for Delay

Bureaucracies with their forms and seemingly endless procedural matters are a cause of delay, not just in foster care drift, but in every important step in the process. We need people who are on a mission to cut through the red tape.

Nowhere are the entangling complications of red tape more obstructive than with interstate adoptions, where the laws and regulations differ between states. Only 71 interstate adoptions among non-relatives were reported by AFCARS in 2003. "It is a national scandal that 25,000 children age out of foster care each year, while waiting adoptive parents are ignored because they are in the wrong state or even the wrong county. It shouldn't be harder for a New Jersey family to adopt a child from Manhattan than from Moscow....The primary reason is that we do not have a national adoption system." (Katz, 2009)

Learning to work together as partners is imperative. If the involved players don't even talk to one another, nothing happens. Effective communication and cooperation are rare skills. Those who care for our most vulnerable citizens need to communicate with one another, to listen, and to be able to work out solutions within "child time."

Perhaps the biggest problem is the unwillingness to share power. When a child is removed from the home for cause, the birth parents are often treated as the problem instead of the solution. The child is made a ward of the court and the caseworker becomes the responsible party. The foster parent may have 24/7 care of the child but has no legal standing. The caseworker, rather than working with either the biological or the foster parents, may be tempted to perceive herself as the sole decision-maker. Gathering input from all sides and cooperation in shaping and working out a plan is the smartest way to achieve the best permanent home available for the child.

The Players

Who are the major players? Seven different parties have important roles to play as the welfare of the child in care is considered and worked out. They are the birth parents, foster parents, caseworkers, the CASA or GAL, mental health professionals, attorneys, and the judge.

Reunification with the **birth parents** in almost all cases is the first goal after removal. Sometimes the birth parents are lulled by inertia or a sense of entitlement. They may think: "This is my child. How dare the state take my child away! They will have to give him back so long as I don't do anything really bad." Instead, the birth parents should demand an early case plan and get started at once on remedying the reasons for removal.

The **foster parents** are the ones providing the day-by-day care. They have the best firsthand knowledge of the child's progress and well-being. Yet they are the only ones without legal standing. This does not make much sense. They are trained professional parents without a significant voice to advocate for the children in their care.

Caseworkers hold the central coordinating position. They have the basic legal responsibility for the placement of the child, convening the players, the development of the case plan, monitoring compliance, and making recommendations to the court. They need to understand the danger of delay and may benefit from additional training in child development.

A **court-appointed special advocate (CASA) or guardian ad litem (GAL)** is often selected by the court to represent the best interests of the child. The court recognizes that the birth parents, foster parents, and caseworkers may all have differing personal agendas. The job of the CASA/GAL is to consider matters from the child's point of view and so inform the court. To do this job well, the CASA/GAL must spend time with the child both in the home and at school. Knowing the child well is critical to providing informed recommendations.

Mental health professionals, while not major players, may have important roles to play. Psychologists and MSW Social Workers may be asked to perform a Bonding Evaluation, a Psychological Evaluation of the birth parents, or an Adoption Home Study. They may be involved in treating the various childhood mental illnesses, including Reactive Attachment Disorder, Adjustment Disorders, Developmental Delay, Learning Disorders, and others. Therapists and psychologists should understand bonding and be current on the latest research to back up their recommendations in court.

Attorneys represent the various parties considering the child's placement options. The welfare department and CASA may each have their own attorneys. The birth parents will (or should) have an attorney. The foster parents may bring an attorney and file a "motion to intervene." And in a competing adoption, the potential parents will each have their own attorneys. What a formula for time-consuming maneuvering and delay! Perhaps it is hoping too much that the attorneys will be eager to serve the child by expediting matters.

The court has the final word. The **judge** has the task of organizing the contestants, considering the many motions, and listening to all the evidence. Finally, the judge must make the decision which will impact and change the child's entire life. The judge must move with both wisdom and relative speed.

Cooperative Adoption

The interests of the child are best served when the major players work together. One special and important possibility where agreement between the parties can override disputes and delays is a cooperative adoption. Birth parents, through a cooperative adoption, can give up parental rights and still retain a legal right to visitation. This can be an ideal way to minimize delay and allow the child to maintain contact with the important people in his or her life.

"Postadoption contact agreements are arrangements that allow for some kind of contact between a child's adoptive family and members of the child's birth family or other persons with whom the child has an established relationship, such as a foster parent, after the child's adoption has been finalized. These arrangements, sometimes referred to as cooperative adoption or open adoption agreements, can range from informal, mutual understandings between the birth and adoptive families to written, formal contracts.

"In general, State law does not prohibit postadoption contact or communication. Since adoptive parents have the right to decide who may have contact with their adopted child, they can allow any amount of contact with birth family members, and such contacts often are arranged by mutual understanding without any formal agreement.

"A written contractual agreement between the parties to an adoption can clarify the type and frequency of the contact or communication and can provide a way for the agreement to be legally enforced. Approximately 23 States currently have statutes that allow written and enforceable contact agreements. The written agreements specify the type and frequency of contact and are signed by the parties to an adoption prior to finalization. The modes of contact can range from an exchange of information about the child between adoptive and birth parents to the exchange of cards, letters, and photos to personal visits with the child by birth family members.

"For the agreements to be enforceable, they must be approved by the court that has jurisdiction over the adoption. Generally, all parties wishing to be included in the agreements must agree in writing to all terms of the agreement prior to the adoption finalization. The court may approve the agreement only if all parties agree on its provisions, and the court finds the agreement is in the best interests of the child." (Child Welfare Information Gateway)

To find information on all of the States and territories, view the complete printable PDF, titled: "Postadoption Contact Agreements Between Birth and Adoptive Families: Summary of state Laws" (www.childwelfare.gov)

Some might fear that a child's stability would be undermined by contact with biological parents after the child has had a permanent adoptive home. Children of divorce, however, maintain contact with both custodial and non-custodial parents, and research shows that the child is the better for maintaining such contact. Others might object that adoptive parents want to adopt a child, not the child's whole biological family. However, cooperative adoption is voluntary and cannot take place unless birth parents and adoptive parents agree in advance on all the terms. Visitation rules can be made very specific to protect the adopting parents.

Cooperative adoption is appropriate when 1) the birth parents and adoptive parents know each other and are willing to enter into a post-adoption agreement; 2) the birth parents realize that they are unable to care for their children but they do not wish to sever all contact with the child for life; and 3) children are in danger of languishing in foster care because reunification is not working, but the situation does not provide grounds for involuntary termination of birth parent rights. By facilitating a voluntary termination of the birth parents' rights, these laws have permitted hundreds of foster children to obtain permanent homes through adoption with minimal delay.

***

Planning for children in temporary care can and should involve the foster parents, the mental health professionals, the caseworker, and the court. How each of these players can help achieve the desired outcome of early permanence in the best and most appropriate home is the focus of the next four chapters.

PART THREE:
WHAT THE MAJOR PLAYERS CAN DO

CHAPTER EIGHT

WHAT THE FOSTER/ADOPT PARENTS CAN DO

> *"One hundred years from now it will not matter what my bank account was, how big my house was or what kind of car I drove. But the world may be a little better because I was important in the life of a child." (Forest Witcraft)*

A Permanent Home

How can foster parents promote permanence? Working to provide a stable home from which a child can grow is the best thing foster parents can do. The first step is to prepare the child for a return to his birth family. Foster parents need to cooperate with visitation. Encourage and support the birth parents as they struggle to remedy the reasons for losing their child. Model and teach parenting skills. Monitor the progress or lack of it toward reunification and keep the caseworker informed.

The foster parents must recognize the critical nature of bonding, and honor that original attachment to the birth parents where appropriate. If the birth parents can remedy the problems that led to the child's removal within a reasonable time, this will maintain the attachment with minimal disruption.

Delay, however, is not an option. Time is not on the side of the child. The child is growing and developing. Childhood is a formative period, not a time to be shifted back and forth. Drift works against nature's clock. Society and the birth parents may feel that they have time, but the child does not. Follow ASFA's wise timelines. Reunify within child time or find a new permanent home.

If and when reunification fails, the foster parents should prepare the child to be adopted, either by kin, by a non-relative, or adopted by themselves. Foster parents adopt 60 percent of foster children who are adopted. Twenty-five percent are adopted by kin.

Foster parents have many ways to actively promote the well-being of their foster child. Four possible interventions will be discussed in this chapter:

1. Preparing a **life book** for the child is an important way to get to know the new arrival and to connect him to his past and, perhaps, his future.

2. By recording daily happenings in a **journal**, the foster parents concretely invest themselves in the child's growth and development. A journal is the strongest record of early events in the child's life. The journal can be critical in defending against unwarranted allegations and in documenting the emergence of bonding for possible adoption. See Appendix G.

3. **Modeling attachment** is an excellent way for foster/adopt parents to confront the emotional isolation that is generated by the temporary nature of foster care.

4. Foster parents need to be **advocates**. This chapter will end with some suggestions on how foster parents can make themselves heard as they advocate for the children in their care.

Preparing a Life Book (Gaunts, 2008)

Each child enters a foster home with cultural differences and considerable emotional baggage. To attach and perhaps bond, the foster family needs to listen to the child; to mentally go where the child is. This is very different from demanding that the child immediately accommodate to his new parents' way of doing things.

How can foster parents "listen" to their new arrival? One good way is to work with the child to prepare a story of the child's past. Called a Life Book, this is wonderful way to give the child an appreciation of his or her past. At the same time, the new parents are learning what the child brings to the present moment.

Life Books create connections. Connections with our past are what give us our identity, stability, wholeness, a sense of permanence. Connections allow us to enter new relationships as a complete person, without feeling so lost and adrift, and without feeling empty. Connections are relationships, memories, feelings, places, and things that make up the fabric of belonging to and being a part of a family or a group. Connections are essential to us because they help define who we are and help provide the foundation for our well-being.

If your foster child is returning to the birth home, you want to maintain and honor as many home connections as you are allowed. Simple connections that make a difference for children are continuing their religious tradition, maintaining the parent's preference for their child's hair style, and including the child's favorite types of food at dinner. In this case the Life Book would be a collection of pictures, impressions, and feelings collected during the period they were placed in your home.

If you are adopting a foster child or are the foster parent of a child that is being adopted, Life Books help prepare the foster child for adoption. Help your child collect pictures, record memories, and write down his or her feelings. This allows the connection process to begin. The child's past will always be a part of who they are and the Life Book provides an appropriate way to help frame their past in context with their new family.

93

Your child's Life Book might contain five chapters. Start with a standard binder and a clear pocket cover. Let your foster/adoptive child design the insert for the front cover. You should also include envelopes in the back of the binder for your child to collect keepsakes. This provides an opportunity for your child to claim ownership of his or her Life Book. Work with your child and be creative!

Chapter One- Who Me?
a) Baby pictures
b) Important information like copy of birth certificate, birth information (hospital, date of birth, weight, length), social security number, etc.
c) Questions to be answered. What is my favorite food? What do I want to be when I grow up? What makes me happy? What makes me angry? ...and on.

Chapter Two – My Birth Family
a) This chapter should include as many pictures as possible of birth relatives such as mom and dad, grandparents, aunts and uncles, siblings, and other relatives. If no pictures are available, then provide space for your child to draw pictures of their family.
b) You could help them make a family tree.
c) Take a trip and take pictures with your child of their birth homes, schools, play areas, fun spots, etc.
d) Ask them to write their feelings about their birth family. What was your favorite family holiday? What do you miss about your birth home? What would you say to your birth parents? ...and so on.
e) This chapter could include a letter to their birth parents saying good bye.

Chapter Three – My Schools
a) A place for each school grade picture.

    b) A listing of schools attended.
    c) Pictures of teachers or class pictures
    d) An art picture for each grade.
    e) Report cards.
Chapter Four – What Makes Me Tick?
    a) Shot records.
    b) Child's medical history.
    c) List of doctors and professional service providers.
    d) Family medical history.
    e) Special needs information.
Chapter Five – Getting Adopted!?!?
    a) Listing and pictures of previous foster parents.
    b) Questions to answer before meeting adoptive parents. Where would I like to live? What do I think my adoptive parents will be like? What would I like my bedroom to be like?
    c) Questions to answer after moving in. Date when I met my new adoptive parents? Date when I moved in? Date my adoption was finalized?
    d) Pictures of my new family and me!

Memories provide us with a base. We need a base from which to grow. That is what a Life Book does: it provides the displaced child with a tangible foundation. Where he can go depends on where he's been. Give your child the gift of his or her past.

Keeping a Journal (Peter Kenny, Attorney, 2008)

The written word has power. Foster parents need to keep a record. The strongest material you can have in advocating for your foster child is a well-documented daily journal. Keeping a daily journal assists you when advocating for your foster child at case conferences or at court hearings. When opinions are divided, your journal provides you with reasons and documentation for your views. Keeping a journal is the number one way you can help your attorney.

Judges can only make decisions about a child's case plan based on the information presented in court. This information, as presented by the Child Welfare Department or the birth parents, is often incomplete, biased, or just plain wrong. Your foster child depends on you as the most informed person in the courtroom to give the judge accurate information about his or her needs. Your journal can provide critical written evidence which can correct misinformation and bolster your position for what is in the child's best interests. Federal law states that you have the right to present both written and oral evidence to the court.

Include everything in your journal; the more information the better. You never know what problems may develop. Here are some situations where a daily journal is extremely helpful:

- Write down behaviors, good or bad, and any progress made.
- Keep a record of doctor appointments.
- Report on school progress or problems. Keep notes from teachers.
- Write down any requests/communications between you and the case workers.
- Keep a record of visitation with the birth parents.
- Document interactions between the siblings and any behaviors after a visit.
- Document problems to anticipate defending yourself against false allegations of abuse or neglect.
- Document daily family contact to support an adoption which members of the birth family are contesting.

Write on a regular basis, daily or at least every few days. Set a regular time to write and stick to it. If you decide to write when you get around to it, the days will fly by and nothing will be recorded. Be sure to write when your foster child has had some special event in his or her life. Be sure to date your journal entries, day, month and year, at the start of each entry. The date can be important should a dispute arise at a later time.

Do not use your journal to attack the birth parents, the Child Welfare Department or any other interested parties. Instead pretend you are a camera, and record what happened each day. Did the child cry, laugh, get angry, act out, appear sad? Describe any actions of the child which lead to your conclusion: failing to eat, unexplained sickness or vomiting; fighting with another child in the household; destructive behavior of any kind. Describe the good things as well: school successes, kindnesses, good interactions with peers. Remember...facts, not feelings.

School Datebooks has produced "A Daily Journal for Foster Parents." This book is a handy way for foster parents to keep regular notes. The book is inexpensive and contains much additional information of value to foster parents. See Appendix G.

Modeling Attachment

The temporary nature of foster care has understandably taught most children to keep a distance. They may seem isolated, avoid contact with others, resist comforting, act cruelly to animals and other children. Parents may find it hard to relate to a child day in and day out without any emotional response. The child's failure to respond is hard to take. Despite these difficulties foster parents can help to

97

prepare the child for permanency and for life by modeling healthy relationships and interactions within the family.

The best time to teach or demonstrate attachment is when the detached or hurtful behavior occurs. The window of opportunity has opened. The unattached child may behave cruelly, or in a way that shows he has no compassion or feeling for others. His antenna fails to pick up the emotions of those around him. This is a teachable moment.

Love the pet: Lori's four-year-old son liked to hurt animals. She caught him hurting the cat. So she took the cat and held it. She showed him how to stroke and love the cat appropriately. She took his hand and said: "This is how we love the cat and not hurt the cat."

If the parent is consistent, the child will get it. When he goes to touch the animal, be sure to say, "Remember, we love the cat, not hurt the cat."

Show me the blood: Jan's daughter fell off her bike and cut her leg open. She was bleeding. Her eight-year-old son was laughing. He got his emotions mixed up sometimes and was not sensitive to others. At this moment Jan said, "Do you see your sister? Do you see her blood? This is not a laughing moment. This is a sad moment. Sissy is crying. Sissy is bleeding. Sissy is hurt. We are sad." Jan's face was sad.

Give him the LOOK: Over-dramatizing facial expressions when explaining emotion to the younger child is compelling. Show him a sad face. Emphasize facial expressions when making a point. Let him get the emotional message from the tone of voice and the look.

The quiet table: Time-outs and isolation for an "unattached" child are counter-productive. In fact, isolation may worsen the detachment. Linda made a quiet table. When she needed a break, or was trying to make dinner, or when trying to stop a behavior, she asked her foster daughter to go to the quiet table. The quiet table was not an isolated place to which the foster daughter disappeared, but a place in the room where everyone else was available. At the quiet table, she had a basket on the floor next to her with quiet things to do. Placed in the basket were coloring books, puzzles, head phones, etc. She kept her foster daughter away from the TV. Her daughter was not allowed to leave the quiet table without permission.

Linda's plan is a good alternative to punishment and does not require the child to go off alone. Having a quiet box in the car to take to church or to the store is a similar idea. It allows for an immediate response when undesirable behavior is exhibited, without disconnecting the child from social interaction.

Show me the move: Defiant behavior is very hard to handle. For long-term help in this area, Sue found that Karate or Tae Kwon Do worked very well, both for teaching self-discipline and stopping problem behavior. Children get their energy out; they learn "yes sir" and "yes m'am;" and they can earn belts and other rewards for progress. When they are hyper or need to refocus attention, Sue simply asked to see their karate moves. This way, she defused the situation and refocused them on another physical and interpersonal activity.

Socks and songs: Brenda's favorite way to interrupt problem behavior was sock-sorting. When her first-grade son who suffered from Reactive Attachment Disorder (RAD) got in trouble, she had him sit at the dining room table and sort socks while she cooked dinner. While he sorted socks, they made up silly songs about the socks and sang. This may not seem like a punishment, but it got him out of the problem situation and allowed mother to spend personal time with him.

Cuddle the baby: Lori got a foster baby through the welfare department. The baby was not even home for a few hours when her older adopted son decided to pick the baby up by its neck. In response, she took the baby and said: "No! We need to love the baby." She started from scratch. This was a live baby, not the cat! Rather than let him handle the baby directly, she bought her son a "Baby Alive" doll that ate, drank, and wet. She added a diaper bag. As Lori would feed or change the real baby, her son copied what she did with his doll. She modeled baby love while reiterating how to love the baby. "This is how we hold the baby; and this is how we feed the baby." After a while, when she was holding the baby, she would let him hold the bottle, or bring baby wipes when she was changing the baby. This was a good way to bond with her son and for him to learn that the new addition to the family was not a threat.

Text me: Kathy's ten-year-old adopted daughter had attachment issues. She was not unattached but was too attached. She could not be apart from her new mother for very long. They worked up to her being away from home for a couple of days. How? The daughter called her mother or texted her when she was feeling alone. She also had a special talking doll that she took places with her. She got this doll at the "Build a Bear" Workshop. Kathy put her own recording inside the bear. To hear the message, her daughter would squeeze the bear's stomach. The recorded message said: "I miss my baby girl. I will see you again soon," followed by Kathy singing: "You are my Sunshine." Also, before her daughter left to stay somewhere, Kathy gave her a verbal itinerary of exactly where she would be. This may sound like a lot of work, but Kathy felt it was the first step toward independence. She put notes in her daughter's school lunch to let her know that mom was okay and could not wait until she got home. Kathy told her daughter regularly that she loved her. This helped her daughter make it through the day in school.

Show me feelings: Mary had a poster in their home that had funny exaggerated faces expressing all varieties of feelings. She asked her son to identify his feeling (or someone else's) by pointing at the proper face on the chart. This was an important way to help him visualize emotion. Mary also asked him to identify his emotion when he woke up in the morning, after school, and before he went to bed. If his emotion changed, it opened a line of communication to discuss what happened.

Children with attachment problems often require extra assistance. If time passes and the child remains unattached, professional help may be needed. Find a good psychologist. Join a support group. Remember, however, that attachment is not a skill learned in a doctor's office but can occur naturally in the home. Most important, parents need to be creative with children who have emotionally distanced themselves. There are no simple solutions to these disorders and no magic pills. Do not be afraid to be unconventional. Just find what works and stick with it. These children are challenging.

A Voice for Foster Parents

"I don't think that the family therapy is helping," said one foster parent. "We all have to go three times a week. We'd do better if it were changed or stopped. But I'm afraid to bring it up or argue for fear we'll have our foster children removed – or be blackballed from any more placements."

In addition to decisions about counseling, foster parents often have something to say about medical care, school issues, visitation with the birth parents, and whether and when to change the permanency plan to adoption. Their knowledge and opinions need to be heard. But unfortunately, fearing retaliation, they are too often afraid to speak out.

Foster children would benefit from an honest discussion of alternatives. Yet, the foster parents may feel they are "just foster parents," or that they are not important decision-makers. Although the 1997 federal Adoption and Safe Families Act (ASFA) said foster parents should be heard in court, they have had little real power.

Caving in meekly to what the others recommend or being silent in fear of retaliation must not be an option. Rather, foster parents must learn how to present their knowledge and opinions without threatening the other players. One does not have to be combative to be effective.

Knowledge is power, and therein lies the foster parents' elemental strength. They must find effective ways to present this everyday knowledge about the child to those who make the critical decisions. Foster parents cannot mandate or order their information to be implemented. Rather, they must act as salesmen in presenting what they know and believe.

Here are nine rules that will help foster parents advocate more effectively for the youngsters under their care.

1. Communicate with the caseworker on a regular, even weekly, basis. Foster parents should not wait for a crisis. Stay in touch. A phone call, a mailed journal update, or an email may be sufficient. Build a normal and steady routine of contact.

2. Keep a daily journal. Record school successes and failures, medical concerns and doctor appointments, and positive and negative behavior. Note how visitation with the birth parents went. The foster parent may add his or her own opinions and judgments, but should keep these separate from the factual information.

3. Begin all communications on a positive note. Good communicators begin with positive remarks. Every face-to-face contact with the other players should start with two uncritical comments or compliments. This tried-and-true strategy is used in mediation, labor-management negotiations, and sales. Praise the other party's office décor or what they are wearing. Offer a smile. Ask a question about something of theirs that you notice, perhaps a family picture or a sports trophy. Thank them for the invitation.

4. Use "I" messages. All good communication must be informative. Foster parents are experts on what they themselves think and feel, not what they suspect the other person thinks. Practice using "I" instead of "you" in your discussions. The "I" message avoids criticism and judgments about other points of view. People are more apt to hear what the foster parents have to say if they don't spend their time attacking the other opinions.

5. Listen. Keep an open mind. Consider what others have to offer. Respect their thinking. People are more likely to listen if they are listened to.

6. Work regularly with the CASA or GAL. Keep the CASA/GAL informed of the everyday progress and setbacks. Use the communication techniques outlined in rules 3-5 above.

7. Work with the birth parents. Remember, reunification must be the initial goal. Foster parents should treat the birth parents with courtesy, cooperate with visitation, and help them learn how to parent when possible. Birth parents can

make good allies if later the foster parents wish to adopt the child.

8. Stand up for the child. The foster parent should state what he or she thinks is best and why. Don't blame or impugn the motives of others. Find a way to get information to the caseworker and, if necessary, into court before the judge. Don't be hesitant for fear of being blackballed. Remember, the best decisions can only be made if all sides and opinions are adequately presented.

9. Regard court as a last resort. The courtroom is an adversarial setting. Arguing in court may sometimes be necessary, but it is far better to have matters resolved before going to court. If foster parents feel they will have problems presenting important information in court, they should hire an attorney who is familiar with foster care policies and laws.

***

Getting along is the key to making a difference. Foster parents should use good communication skills to be sure that the information necessary to make informed decisions affecting the child's entire life and future is available to the welfare department and in court.

Children in care need the foster parents' knowledge and love. They also need the foster parent to stand up as an advocate. Foster parents must make every effort to get along with those in power. If the foster parents are concerned that the child's best interests are still being ignored, they should continue with their role as advocate. They may need to hire an attorney to be sure that all information and recommendations are fully presented before the judge. The child is the most important party to all these efforts, and the child's best interests are paramount.

CHAPTER NINE

THE ROLE OF THE MENTAL HEALTH PROFESSIONAL

To bridge the emptiness
in search of psychic pain
with grace to reach inside a troubled soul
To heal the mind and heart
and bridge the loneliness of discontent
That is my grace and gift

A mental health professional (psychologist, psychiatrist, or social worker) can play three important roles on the foster child's road to bonding and permanence. A correct diagnosis is necessary to get started. Then treatment may be necessary to address one of the many psychiatric disorders to which foster children are particularly vulnerable. Finally, the mental health professional can attest to the presence or absence of bonding by performing a bonding evaluation.

Diagnosis

Obtaining the correct diagnosis through a Childhood Mental Status Exam is the first step. The most common disorders include Reactive Attachment Disorder (RAD), Oppositional Defiant Disorder (ODD), Attention Deficit/Hyperactivity Disorder (AD/HD), various Learning

Disorders, and Adjustment Disorders. More serious are Conduct Disorders, Major Depression, and Autism. If medications appear appropriate, then a physician or psychiatrist will be needed.

At most, a therapist is likely to spend one or two hours per week with the child. Parents spend 24 hours in a day. What parents do or do not do will have considerably more influence on the child's well-being than what happens in the therapist's office. A wise child therapist will help the parents to become the primary healers.

Children suffering from Reactive Attachment Disorder make parenting exceptionally difficult. Ordinary parent-child communication can be misinterpreted by the child and backfire. The RAD child may shut down emotionally and seem unreachable, not understanding love nor trusting it. For this reason, we will use the following disorder as an example to show how a therapist can help the child by working with and through the parents.

Treating Reactive Attachment Disorder (RAD)

More than with any other mental disorder, the healing for Reactive Attachment Disorder (RAD) takes place in the home. The main job of the therapist is to structure significant connecting with others, especially family members.

In the days of the cold war, when east and west were walled off, a man made daily trips across the border into the east zone with wheelbarrows full of fruit packed in straw. Although the fruit was legitimate, the border guards were certain that the man was a smuggler. For weeks, they checked everything, searched the straw, broke open the fruit, tested wood splinters and pieces of straw for contraband chemicals. One day, the man told them it was his last trip. The guards outdid themselves in checking, but to no avail.

106

Once the man was safely across the border, they asked him if he would reveal what he was smuggling. "We can't sleep at night not knowing." "Of course," the man replied. "I'm smuggling wheelbarrows."

Don't miss the obvious. RAD is not amenable to cognitive behavioral therapy, crisis intervention, nor even to behavior modification. Bonding cannot be forced, but occurs naturally when the stage is set and the time is right. Attachments and bonding happen, not in offices, but out there in the everyday world.

Broken relationships are a major cause of RAD. They lead to hesitance in re-connecting and indifference. The cure involves beginning to trust and learning to share important events over time in daily life, such as eating, sleeping, going places, and playing together.

Meaningful and vital relationships do not take place in artificial environments. They happen in that wonderful mix of emotional entanglements within the family. Five obvious factors should constitute the basis of RAD therapy.

A Permanent Home: The bonding therapist's first job is to make sure the child has a permanent home. Bonding takes place between specific persons. To facilitate bonding with a person likely to disappear is dangerous. Losing a loved one hurts badly. The loss may cause the child to reconsider the risk of future attachments and vote to "opt out." Repeated loss entrenches RAD.

Every child has the right to a permanent home. One might even argue that "permanent" is one of the hidden assumptions built into the idea of "home." The therapist's first job is a social work task: to do everything possible working with the welfare department to further permanence. Help the child remain with the birth parents if possible. Arrange for in-home services. If the child must be removed, work to shorten the time in limbo. Foster care is, or should be, temporary. Help evaluate available kin. Promote concurrent planning to minimize multiple moves. Try to approach every placement away from the birth home as if it could be the last one. Find adoptive parents.

A good therapist realizes that foster parents face a serious dilemma. On the one hand, foster parents are likely to attach, even "fall in love" with the children in their care. On the other hand, if the child trusts and loves them in return and then is moved, trauma results. To anticipate this dilemma, the therapist should do everything possible to prevent or minimize multiple moves, and to shorten the time in temporary care. Bonding therapy should not be attempted in a temporary setting.

Structure Connecting: As soon as a permanent home is established, facilitate the avenues of attachment. Bonding occurs naturally and so should the treatment of RAD. Parents should be counseled to notice at least two extra things about their child each day. The therapist should remind them to smile at their child, and touch, and ask questions. Read or make up bedtime stories. Consider getting a pet to love and be loved by.

Parents of an RAD child should avoid grounding and time-outs as discipline since these procedures tend to isolate and further alienate the child. Instead, keep the child nearby so he or she can interact. Should the child become angry and shout, this is a personal reaction and may actually be a step forward from the detachment of RAD.

Peers are critical partners, perhaps even more than parents. The therapist will advise parents to encourage participation in groups such as 4-H, school clubs and sports, summer baseball, soccer, or the swim team. Be there and cheer them on even if they are not stars. Welcome sleepovers and two-person games on the computer. Parents should be urged to do what they can to provide possibilities for contact with peers, even when that contact involves arguing and disagreements. Bonding has positive and negative aspects, but it cannot happen without the opportunity to interact.

Model Emotions and Compassion: Emotions are personal. Reasoning and logic are not. The therapist should encourage parents to let their own feelings show. Children need to learn that their parents have feelings too. Foster/adopt parents should feel free to laugh with their child. Some things are very funny. It is all right for foster/adopt parents to show their anger too, as long as it does not degenerate into physical violence or personal demeaning.

Crying is okay. I remember when my mother phoned to tell me my father had two major heart attacks and was not expected to live. I dropped the phone, began to cry, and raced around the house frantically to prepare for a quick trip to Chicago. My children were amazed. They had never seen me cry. They responded immediately to my requests for cards to give grandpa. (He recovered.) My relationship with my children deepened.

Therapists can teach parents to use "I" messages. For example: "I am upset with what you have done. I want you to come here and sit next to me for five minutes." Putting parental emotions into words can help the RAD child recognize his or her own feelings. Parents should avoid starting sentences with "you," as this suggests that the parent knows what is going on inside the child. Further, it implies an accusation which the child will probably deny.

Accentuate the Positive: Parents will get more of whatever they pay attention to. Every teacher, parent, and supervisor knows this. People are known to say: "I don't know what's the matter with her. The more I get after her, the worse she gets....She's just doing it to get attention." Of course she is. Attention, whether positive or negative, is a payoff.

The therapist needs to teach parents to brainstorm with each other about times when their child relates personally with others. This is an important way to share awareness about incidents worthy of notice. Pick any event when the child interacts with a companion. When he or she joins a club, has a friend over, or plays with a pet. Especially be aware of incidents such as; getting into an argument or a fight, joining in the family in conversation or action. Then, reward these moments with a comment or a touch; "I'm glad to see you and Nicole together...."I am glad you came with us....." Parents need to encourage these breakthroughs with attention.

Expect Misbehavior: Misbehavior may be problematic but it is, nevertheless, a relationship. Misbehaving is a step forward, away from being a loner, and into the real world of other people. On the road back to normalcy, the RAD child may be disrespectful, lie, fight, steal, break things, and do much else to irritate the parent. They may try a parent's patience to its limit.

The therapist needs to support and encourage parents as they deal with an unruly child. The therapist can teach how to correct these behaviors without squelching the child. Avoid long lectures. Lectures give too much attention to misbehavior and rarely work. The therapist can suggest more appropriate ways to discipline than isolating the RAD child. Instead, focus directly on the lying and stealing and other uncivil behaviors. If the child lies, the discipline might be to refuse to accept his word from then on. If he steals, search his room, pat him down before leaving for school, make him pay back what is pilfered. The goal is to skip the lecture, ignore the bad behavior itself, and accomplish the desired outcome. The lies are stopped because the parents seek other sources for the truth. The stealing is handled because the parents take practical measures to uncover the theft.

While misbehavior may be wearisome to the parents, the therapist can remind them that, for the RAD child, it may represent progress. Parents might even be somewhat pleased that the child is testing them out. The therapist should encourage them to respond personally and directly, without pushing the child away. Failure to attach is the predecessor of psychopathy, the lack of empathy or feeling for others. This is true moral retardation, far more serious than the more common misbehaviors of childhood.

To truly help a child, the parent must go where the child "lives," to the child's personal world view. Giving moralistic admonitions to an RAD child is like trying to provide directions to a location without knowing where the potential traveler is starting out. To get a traveler where he needs to be, one must start where he is. With RAD, the starting point is a lack of empathy or emotion. To heal this, the therapist must help the parent to understand the emotional hurt and resultant anger that underlies the fear to love.

In summary, the therapist might say to the parent: "Open your eyes to the obvious. Accept the real issues that circumscribe RAD. Then be patient. Don't force things. Pass the tests. And most simply of all, just be there."

The Assessment of Bonding

In addition to the roles of diagnostician and therapist, the mental health professional may be asked to assess bonding. The details of bonding are reasonably well elaborated out in the psychological literature, in the guidelines of state welfare departments, and by common sense. As noted in Chapter Two, however, the lack of a clear definition of bonding has led to a smorgasbord of unfocused data-gathering. Too often, assessments have used a variety of

111

processes and techniques rather than focusing on bonding, its definition and its objective criteria.

The first and obvious step in conducting an assessment is to know what you are assessing. The evaluator must have a clear definition of bonding as his template. Then the assessment should answer the simple question: Is this child bonded to these parents? The procedures employed and the data collected should be relevant to answering this question.

A thorough and professional evaluation of bonding will gather information about the child's daily living from five or more sources.

1. Review all available documents, including the foster parents' journal, child welfare records, court documents, reports from physicians, therapists, and other persons with relevant knowledge. In addition to pinpointing the time in the foster/adopt home, these documents and reports should provide information related to the various objective definitions of bonding.

2. Obtain collateral information from extended family members, neighbors, babysitters, teachers, and any others who might have had the opportunity to observe the child with this family. Is the child perceived as a member of the family? The wisdom of the larger community is a valid way to assess bonding.

3. A detailed written developmental history provided by the foster parents will offer data on the child's growth and development, as well as the child's behavior, family situation, and other circumstances. The history can also be offered as evidence on how well the foster/adopt parents know the child, an important demonstration of the reciprocal definition of bonding.

4. Establish a developmental age. A measure of the child's developmental age can be important to document the child's special needs which would qualify the family for post-

adoption subsidies. Equally important, when compared with the child's development at the time of placement, the developmental age can be used to document the child's progress while in the foster/adopt home. A strong argument can be made in court to "let well enough alone." The Vineland Social Maturity Scale is one acceptable test to establish a developmental age. Other equally good checklists and test instruments are available for this purpose.

5. Child behaviors can be documented by various instruments and research-based checklists that demonstrate bonding. Many checklists exist which provide a good review of those behaviors which research has identified to indicate bonding. Two good examples are the Randolph Attachment Disorder Questionnaire (Evergreen Attachment Center in Colorado) and Keck's list of attachment disorders from the Ohio Attachment and Bonding Center. The Groves Bonding Checklist (GBC) includes many of the most important bonding behaviors. (See Appendix F.)

6. Projective techniques can be introduced to elicit emotions below the surface. The child is presented with a neutral but stimulating object or task and asked to respond. Since the stimulus admits of many possible variations, the child must complete the task in his or her own unique way. The evaluator should structure the situation so that the stimulus will evoke a response about relationships and personal connections.

    a) Drawings are a popular procedure. The authors use a series of three drawings with no leading hints. The child is requested in order to: "Draw Anything. Draw a Whole Person. Draw Your Family." Obviously, it is of interest whom the child places in his or her family and who is next to whom. Drawings could also be requested to show the child interacting with siblings or with any and all of the significant adults.

b) Stories are also helpful. The evaluator may suggest a family theme. Or show the child evocative pictures about relationships and request imaginative stories. Magazine ads that suggest attachment and family issues might be used to elicit stories.

c) Sentence completion tests are frequently used to extract hidden feelings. The evaluator asks the child to complete a series of neutral phrases. The half-sentences should reflect the evaluator's desire to learn more about the child's relationships. Opening fragments such as "I am____" "I am afraid____" "I am happy when____" "I wish____" "My family is____" "I don't care____" "My dad____" "My mom____" The possibilities for encouraging useful information about the child's ability to connect are limited only by the imagination of the evaluator.

7. First-hand observation of the child in the presence of the foster/adopt family is essential. The evaluator might meet with the entire family for several hours in his or her office playroom. While discussing the situation with family members, the evaluator has the opportunity to observe the interactions between the child and family members in free play. A visit to the home is even more informative.

8. A semi-structured dyadic interview can be quite helpful by moving beyond free play. Stokes and Strothman (1996) routinely set some specific parent-child tasks. The parent may be asked to groom the child, to teach the child something new, to share a small meal, to leave and come back, to play a game together, to discuss something important or difficult, to make up a story together, to plan an activity together, and so on. The evaluator then has the opportunity to observe what happens in specific situations.

Once the information has been collected, a written report should follow. The presentation of a meal is as important as the food itself, as any good chef will attest. The same is true of a Bonding Assessment. The evaluator must present a clear and well-organized report. Writing a good report and presenting the factual information in a concise and compelling way is the other half of conducting a thorough evaluation. The evaluator must take as much care to write a thorough report as he or she did to conduct the evaluation.

The welfare department and the court will make their decisions based in good part upon the written report. The evaluator's report should be available for the judge to review after his or her memory of the oral testimony may have faded. Judges read. A well-documented, objective, fact-focused, written report to the court is very important.

A good written bonding assessment has six parts: problem, methods, results, discussion, conclusion, and research.

The report should begin with a brief statement of the problem, noting that the family has had the child in the home for a specified period of time, and that the family wishes to provide this child with a permanent home through adoption.

A list of the materials reviewed and the procedures accomplished should follow in the methods section.

The section on results should define bonding, giving research support for the definition and sub-definitions. The four specific ways to define bonding mentioned in Chapter Two should be fleshed out with the factual evidence provided by the data obtained in conducting the actual assessment. The facts should be allowed to speak for themselves. The bonding evaluator needs to line up the data in relation to the four operational definitions of bonding.

Time together: How long have the parents and child been living together?

Behavior: What behaviors does the child show?

Reciprocity: How do the parent and child interact? What long-term commitments are the parties willing to make to each other?

Community perception: What does the community think?

The discussion section may contain the reflections of the evaluator. Opinion should be reserved for this section and kept separate from the facts.

In the conclusion to the evaluation, a simple statement should be added stating whether bonding has or has not occurred.

If bonding has occurred, the research and current statistics should be provided at the end of the report, telling what happens when bonded relationships are severed. The younger the child is, the more lasting and destructive the consequences of termination can be. Removing a child from bonded relationships has been compared to the loss of a spouse, brain surgery, or the death of a parent. The written report should indicate that the research is unequivocal in statistically documenting a dramatic increase in childhood and adult psychiatric disorders following the loss of a bonded relationship. Reactive attachment disorder, developmental delay, oppositional defiant disorder, AD/HD, and learning disorders have all been linked to disruptions of bonding and may occur soon after such a loss. Sometimes, however, the impact is delayed and shows up in later life with an increase in the likelihood of adult mental illness, homelessness, crime, and poverty.

Bonding has been defined and the serious consequences that may occur when it is interrupted have been presented. Now it is time to go to the welfare departments and courts, those institutions that are trusted by society to watch out for foster children.

CHAPTER TEN

HOW THE CHILD WELFARE DEPARTMENT CAN HELP

> *"Those who make the laws and those who administer and enforce them must acknowledge that the consistent day-to-day loving and guiding parental relationship that a child needs to mature and grow into a wholesome and law-abiding citizen can be provided by psychological or adoptive parents just as effectively as by biological parents." (Ketcham, 1998)*

The primary legal responsibility for foster children lies with the state. Foster children are technically "wards of the court" under the guardianship of the child welfare department and their caseworkers. The child welfare department has the power to make and change policies and the responsibility to see that the laws and policies are followed. More than any of the other major players, the child welfare department can facilitate the ultimate goal: assuring safety and achieving permanence within one year.

A major cause of foster care drift is the failure to recognize that meeting the foster child's need for permanence is paramount. Too often, caseworkers take an unwarrantedly long time to provide the birth parents with additional chances. They assume that the child is in a safe home while time runs on, playing back and forth between the needs of the biological parents, the foster/adopt parents, and often in last place, the needs of the child. Children are reunited with birth parents repeatedly, only to be removed once again when birth parents are unwilling or unable to care for the child. Yet only half of all foster children ultimately return home to stay. Delaying to "get it right" becomes a silent but very real form of child abuse.

Bureaucracy is another major cause of delay. The system has many rules and many players: child welfare departments, child protection services, private child welfare agencies, the courts, specialists and therapists, guardians ad litem, court-appointed special advocates, the birth parents, and the foster parents. Each party may have its own vested interests and its own attorney. When one party sees waiting as an advantage or fears losing, that party may use the time-tested legal strategy of continuances and postponement. The child is harmed by delay, yet rarely does anyone represent the child's right to a timely solution.

The child welfare system is beset with workers who are undertrained and overburdened. Turnover is high. Attention is necessarily focused on the more problematic children. Children who have food, a roof over their heads and no reported problems are often ignored and left to drift in foster care.

Recommended Policy Changes

Child welfare departments make policies for caseworkers to put into action. Here are some overall principles and policy recommendations which would help shorten the time in foster care and move the train toward permanence.

Classify foster homes into three simple categories: (1) Foster Homes Open to Adoption; (2) Purely Temporary Foster Homes; (3) Homes Open to both Temporary and Permanent Possibilities. When reunification seems unlikely at the start, the child can be placed from the start in a home which offers a permanency alternative. Moves can be kept to a minimum.

Keep detailed public statistics: The availability of county-by-county and statewide statistics on reunifications, adoptions, and emancipations would hold welfare departments accountable to scrutiny. Interested parties could note the average length of time spent in foster care, and which counties appeared to be doing a better job. By documenting successes and failures, the child welfare departments might be motivated to work more diligently to find permanent solutions.

Reverse the financial gain for licensed child-placing agencies handling children in foster care. Make it less and less rewarding to keep a child in care after 12 months, or as adolescence approaches. After a child turns 10, begin lowering the amount incrementally that the agency receives, and offer a bonus for safe and appropriate permanence.

Rethink home-finding for children in care, especially older children. Nearly one-half of foster children are eleven or older and about one-fifth are over fifteen. (Shirk et al, 2004) More than redoubling our efforts, we need to seek out new ways to search for possible permanent homes. Pat O'Brien in New York ("You Gotta Believe") offers one such approach. His agency finds permanent homes for children 10 and older. Instead of starting with the available pool of approved foster homes, he begins with the young person. "Whom do you like? Who likes you?" It might be a grandma, a neighbor, the child's teacher, probation officer, coach, therapist, or the parent of a friend. That person will get a call. They are told of the young person's attachment, and are invited to a weekly meeting. If the adult is interested, the process of foster parent licensing might begin. This is a reversal of the usual way homes are found. YGB begins with the interests of

119

the child rather than searching the list of already available foster families.

Caseworkers Can Make a Difference

To benefit the child, foster care needs to be brief. The best time and place to begin to follow the deadlines is right away. A plan to achieve permanency should begin immediately upon removal from the problem home. A case plan can and should be developed within a day or two. The reunification plan should state specific tasks and standards which the legal parents must meet in order to be reunited with their child. Adoption can be planned from the start as an alternative should the family reunification plan fail.

Here are eleven obvious actions that can shorten the time in foster care without in any way jeopardizing the child's need for a safe and secure home.

Listen to the birth parents and foster parents. The parents, not the caseworker, are the important players. "Hear" not only their words but their behavior. Are they doing what they promised?

Learn about the critical importance of bonding and permanence. Know what bonding means and what happens when it is interrupted. Acknowledge the fact that every child has the right to a permanent home.

Maintain the birth home without removing the child when possible. If necessary to guarantee safety, provide regular in-home services.

Start immediately. Within 24 hours of removal, the caseworker should be able to provide the birth parent(s) with a case plan showing them how to remedy the abuse or neglect. This is not brain surgery. What the caseworker needs to do is directly address the problems that led to the removal. If the housing is substandard, the birth parents must find new housing. If the parents have little parenting skill or the child was left alone, require parent training classes. If a boyfriend abused the child, get rid of the boyfriend. If one or both parents were on drugs, they may need to pass a few random drug screens. And so on. See Appendix E for a sample format of an early case plan. The caseworker should take the initial working plan to the judge and get it "baptized" by court order.

Revise the case plan. As new information becomes available, make the appropriate changes or additions. The caseworker and the judge will then have the additional information about early compliance. The clock will already have been ticking, either on the way to reunification or toward termination.

Monitor the case plan weekly. No better way exists to obtain compliance than to check personally each week. Are the birth parents doing what is necessary for the return of their child? Regular monitoring builds a strong case for or against reunification.

Locate any relatives within two weeks. One major cause of delay is the eleventh-hour relative, sometimes referred to as kin-come-lately. Just when a termination of parental rights is about to happen, an unattached relative from far away emerges; an uncle, a grandmother, or a half-sibling. This throws a monkey wrench into the mix. The proceedings come to a halt while this new matter is being considered. An immediate and thorough search for potential relative placements will avoid this delay.

Follow the federal deadlines. The court generally reviews the status of children in care every three months. If the birth parents do not appear to be making a reasonable effort for reunification by six months, the permanency plan can be changed to adoption. Federal law (ASFA) requires that a termination of parental rights be filed after 12-15 months of out-of-home care. These deadlines are vitally important and

121

need to be honored. Include specific "markers" indicating progress or the lack of it. Stick to facts. This is important to replace vague caseworker notes indicating the opinion that mother has a better attitude.

Avoid unnecessary moves. Every placement of a foster child should be made as if it were the last. Patterns of connecting are formed and solidified in the child's personality, only to be disrupted if and when a move is made.

Implement concurrent planning.
Concurrent planning is nothing more than contingency arrangements for a "rainy day." If we were to plan a picnic, we would usually have an alternative in case it rained. We do this for all important matters. To avoid delay, the caseworker must make a fallback plan, a second choice, something else to implement if and when the primary effort at reunification fails. Our vulnerable children deserve at least that much.

Eliminate emancipation to independent living as a permanency plan. Six percent of foster children have their permanency plan listed as independent living. Independent living is not a permanency plan. Rather, it is an outrageous formula for failure.

PART FOUR:
GOING TO COURT

CHAPTER ELEVEN

COURTS HAVE THE FINAL WORD

"Justice delayed is justice denied."
(William Gladstone, British Prime Minister)

Presenting Bonding in Court

"We have had Briana for 19 months, since she was five weeks old," related Jan Craft, foster mom. "We asked our caseworker if we could adopt her, but the caseworker told us that the parental rights had not yet been terminated. As soon as that happened, an elderly grandmother from several states away expressed an interest in adopting Briana. Grandmother had never seen her. We have become very attached to Briana and she to us. She has lived with us for almost her entire life. We love her and want to continue to be her parents." The Crafts can pursue their wish to adopt Briana in court. While the termination and adoption may be disputed, bonding is on their side and will be a key issue in the court hearing.

Hiring an Attorney

Foster parents know the most about the children in their care and have the most to offer in terms of possible permanence. They must express their own rights and wishes, but more importantly, they must advocate for the children in their home. Many foster parents are hesitant to speak out for fear of being labeled as troublemakers. In fact, foster parents who are appropriately assertive are more apt to be fully heard. They would be wise to hire an attorney as soon as they wish to adopt, before matters get set in cement.

When hiring an attorney, foster/adopt parents want someone who is knowledgeable and experienced in the area of their concern. Whether incorporating a business, planning an estate, or suing for personal injury, one wants to be represented by someone who has expertise in that particular area. The same applies to adoptions from foster care. Foster parents need an attorney who is familiar with the state and federal laws. The attorney should also be familiar with agency and state policies and know the people in the system. Every state has thick policy manuals which cover such topics as bonding, adoption, subsidies, and a definition of special needs.

The attorney needs to understand bonding. While the varied legal procedures must be followed conscientiously, the presentation and proof of bonding between the child and the foster/adopt parents may be the strongest argument for keeping them together; especially in a contested adoption. Bonding, when it occurs, is critical to a child's development. The disruption of a demonstrated bonded relationship does considerable damage which may be irreversible. The problem for an attorney is to present proof of bonding and the consequences of its disruption to the court in a factual and evidentiary way.

The Attorney's Role

Foster parents need a knowledgeable attorney as soon as they have decided to adopt. Here are some things an attorney can do after the child has been in a potential adoptive foster home for six months or more.

Review the state case conference policy with the foster parents. Foster parents in many states have the right to call a case conference anytime they believe the current case plan is not serving the best interests of their foster child. If they believe that efforts toward reunification have been exhausted, they can propose changing the permanency plan from reunification to adoption.

The attorney may wish to accompany the foster parents to the case conference to assure that policies and laws are followed.

The attorney may wish to consult with the foster child's CASA or GAL about the foster child's best interests and permanency plan. Foster parents have a stronger case when all parties representing the child are working toward the same goal.

The attorney can advise the foster parents about the federal laws, the state laws, and child welfare policies related to foster care and adoption, including any eligibility for post-adoption subsidies.

The attorney can consult with county and state officials to help resolve any disagreements between the concerns of the foster parents and the welfare department.

The attorney will want to attend all court hearings with the foster parents to make certain that they have the full say to which the law entitles them.

The attorney may file for adoption. Under certain circumstances, the attorney may recommend filing for adoption before there has been a termination of parental rights (TPR.) The law may allow for the adoption and the TPR to be handled together when this serves the child's best interests.

The attorney may wish to ask the court to order a bonding evaluation.

The attorney will apply for all the post-adoption subsidies for which the foster/adoptive parents are eligible.

Foster parents will probably not have legal standing, unless they have filed to adopt. Depending on the state, foster parents may or may not have other lesser legal rights. These lesser rights include the right to notification of all periodic review hearings, the right to present a written statement to the court, the right to testify, and the right to cross-examine the caseworker and all other witnesses at the hearing. If foster parents do not have legal standing, their attorney's first step would then be to file a "motion to intervene."

Most foster children who are adopted are adopted by their foster parents. For attorneys, such adoptions are complicated. Multiple parties have legal standing including the welfare department. Before an adoption petition can be filed, multiple meetings and hearings are involved, including case conferences and appeals, initial court hearings, review hearings, permanency hearings, and the termination of parental rights. In certain instances, agreements may need to be achieved so a cooperative adoption can take place. Finally, if the child qualifies as having "special needs," four different post-adoption subsidies from different sources may be available at the federal or state level. These subsidies must be arranged before the adoption is finalized.

Bonding Must Be Clearly Defined

The extensive research defining bonding has been laid out in Chapter Two. In the following paragraphs, bonding is defined in ways that the attorney can use effectively in court. The dictionary defines bonding as a unique relationship between two people, enduring for a long time, even a lifetime.

Based upon a thorough review of the research in Chapter Two, we have expanded this definition and are repeating it here.:

Bonding is a significant reciprocal attachment which both parties want and expect to continue, and which is interrupted or terminated at considerable peril to the parties involved. Humans bond by sharing important daily life events over time, everyday events such as eating, sleeping, and playing together.

Legislation, case law, and research provide more detailed and specific definitions which we have also presented earlier. We are repeating them here. Any one of the following standards is sufficient to verify bonding.

Welfare policy: Family identification is a standard contained in the Child Welfare Manuals of many states. As state policy, this definition carries legal weight. It calls on the collective wisdom of the extended family, the school, neighbors, the church, even the work place. How does the larger community view the relationship? Do they perceive this child as a member of the foster/adopt family?

Federal and state law: Time in place is a factual way to measure bonding. In a parent-child setting, bonding is likely after three months, probable after six and almost certain after 12 months. This definition is reflected in both federal and state laws. (See Appendices A and B.)

The federal Adoption and Safe Families Act (ASFA, 1997) provides a strong legal argument in favor of bonding, even over blood kinship. When it can be proven, bonding outweighs kinship. In his or her brief, the attorney can cite all of the three-, six-, and 12-month timelines contained in federal and state laws as evidence of the legislative concern that bonded relationships be honored. Further, the attorney can make the point that the law is designed to protect the most vulnerable party, in this case, the child. The right of the child to physical and mental health and safety supersedes all other rights, including the right of the birth parents to possession. The child's best interest comes first. "The new statute now stresses that the child's health and safety shall be the paramount concern in determining what is reasonable, and consistent with the plan for timely permanent placement of a child." (ASFA Summary, www.casanet.org).

Case law: Many appellate court decisions have favored the preservation of in disputed permanent placements. The precise written language used by these courts defines bonding legally and can be brought to the attention of trial courts. Appellate court language may be used as a standard. For a list of recent appellate court decisions, see Appendix C.

Behavior: The behavior of the child is another way to determine whether bonding has occurred. Behaviors such as copying adult mannerisms and habits, interest and attentiveness, physical contact, joy, appropriate protest and anger, and the need to stay close (among many other behaviors) have been shown to document the presence of bonding. Developmental and psychological research heavily supports this definition. The Groves Bonding Checklist in Appendix F can be completed by a mental health professional and presented in court.

Lifetime commitment: Bonding is reciprocal. Still another way to measure bonding is to present and evaluate the promise expressed by the actual or potential parents. Foster parents have already demonstrated their day-to-day commitment. They know what they are getting into, and their stated wish to become a lifetime parent reflects the "chemistry" that has emerged between the child and the foster/adopt parents.

The attorney's first task in court is to have an expert present a clear and objective definition of bonding. While all the definitions of bonding carry weight, it may be best to use the policy and legal definitions as a primary definition.

Display the actual written standard, once it has been determined, on a poster for everyone in the courtroom to see while witnesses are led through their testimony point by point. This can be quite effective. A good attorney will ask the expert whether mere kinship, visitation, and other part-time contact can result in bonding.

One final caution on the definition of bonding is needed. Some naïve persons believe that the child who has bonded well to one family is a "good bonder" and will do equally well if moved. The child appears pleasant and compliant, showing no overt signs of distress. As explained in Chapter Two, this is correctly called "pseudo-bonding" and reflects the opposite of true bonding. The Diagnostic and Statistical Manual of the American Psychiatric Association describes this indiscriminate attachment and sociability as one form of "Reactive Attachment Disorder." (DSM-IV-TR, 2005)

Expert Testimony: The Mental Health Professional as Witness

The Children's Law Center and the Judicial Education Center in New Mexico have published a "Child Welfare Handbook (2007)" to educate judges, attorneys, and caseworkers on facilitating the child's path from abuse to permanence. The purpose and importance of a bonding study are described in Chapter 37.13: "A bonding study should stand alone and be requested because it makes a unique contribution. The bonding issue in permanency planning is the extent to which the parent is capable of caring for the child from the perspective of bonding and attachment. The bonding study draws data from observation, from social and interpersonal reports, and from cognitive and emotional assessments." More details about how to perform a thorough

131

and presentable bonding assessment are provided in Chapter Nine.

A psychologist or other expert witness on bonding should be available to testify on the results of the assessment. (See Chapter Nine.) The attorney should qualify the evaluator as an expert witness on bonding, then walk him or her through the report, detailing each proof of bonding, asking specifically if the child exhibits the types of behavior which would satisfy the definition's components, presenting the statistics on what happens when bonding is interrupted, and asking the expert for an opinion as to whether bonding has occurred.

Scholarly articles on bonding can and should be presented to the court to educate the judge about these matters. These articles may be included as part of the expert's testimony, and should include research on the harm done when bonded relationships are interrupted. Many such articles are listed in the Reference section of this book. The foster parents' attorney should be aware of the rules of evidence in the relevant jurisdiction to ensure that such articles can withstand anticipated objections and be admitted into evidence.

The Foster/Adopt Parent as Witness

Keeping a journal, as explained in Chapter Eight, is the number one way foster parents can help their attorney present a compelling argument. Foster parents should prepare for court by reviewing the written material in their journal entries. The Daily Journal for Foster Parents (2008) contains a helpful quarterly summary outline of important issues. This summary can be used to inform the judge at a court review hearing, to update the caseworker in preparation for a case conference, or simply to organize the parent's own thinking about their foster child. See Appendix D for a copy of the summary outline. Other written materials might also be entered in the summary.

Courts are adversarial settings and can be intimidating. The foster/adopt parent may be concerned about being cross-examined. The attorney might reassure and counsel the foster/adopt witness in the following manner: "You are on the stand to express what you think is best for the child in your care. Keep it simple. Think of the child's welfare and try not to worry about yourself. Don't be rushed. Take your time to answer any questions. It's okay to admit that you don't know something. Don't badmouth the birth parents or any other party. Stay positive in expressing your feelings about the child."

The attorney should ask for a declaration of the foster/adopt parents' commitment. The foster/adopt parents should make clear to the court that they understand adoption to be a promise of forever. They are offering the child a permanent home.

The foster parents' attorney may choose to call members of the community who have observed first-hand the day-to-day interactions between child and family. While these witnesses cannot offer an expert opinion, they can be led through the bonding standards point by point.

The Role of the CASA/GAL

Often, the court will appoint a special advocate to represent the best interests and rights of the foster child. The court-appointed special advocate (CASA) or guardian ad litem (GAL) is specially trained and has legal standing. Their job is to talk to all parties, especially the foster child, and make recommendations to the court.

The role of the CASA or GAL becomes more important when the foster parent and the welfare department have conflicting views or interests. The welfare department may feel strongly about following certain policies, saving the state money, and/or supporting the opposing adoption petition of another party. The foster parents may have a different opinion about what they perceive to be the child's best interests. They may want to adopt the child against the continuing wishes of the birth parents.

When disagreements occur, the court may welcome a third opinion, especially when the CASA or GAL has obtained firsthand information through home visits. The foster parents and welfare departments may both woo the CASA/GAL for support.

The Court Has Problems

The courts which oversee the foster care system are overcrowded. To move a child from foster care to permanence within 12 months, court hearings are needed upon entering the foster care system and every three to six months thereafter. Instead, cases may wait months even for the initial hearing. Furthermore, the legal rules for the presentation of evidence frequently fail to admit pertinent information. Complicated family matters are often poorly presented and inadequately resolved in court.

More courts at all levels are recognizing the importance of bonding when making placement decisions. This consideration, however, remains far from universal. Many courts still fail to consider the documented bond between the foster parent and foster child and choose adoptive placement with a long lost relative, relying solely on the primacy of biological rights. Thanks to the Adoption and Safe Families Act (ASFA), the rights of the child are or should be considered paramount.

Regulatory and statutory barriers exist to complicate the adoption of foster children who cannot return to their parents' homes. The separate and sometimes conflicting requirements between the regulations that govern foster care and adoption can slow the process. Examples of statutes that can delay matters include:

Vague laws that can be misinterpreted to require sequential, rather than concurrent planning, thus greatly lengthening the time a child spends in foster care.

- Statutes that fail to consider the child's developmental needs in establishing reunification time lines.
- Laws that allow the establishment of a plan for long-term foster care.
- Statutes that require that reunification services be given to birth parents who do not want them.
- Policies that value blood relatives and remove children from homes where they have significantly bonded, to place them with heretofore unknown siblings and relatives.

Court delays are endemic. Continuances present a problem. The courts may allow continuances to give the birth parents chance after chance. Perhaps the parties have not been properly notified. Or another court case must be heard. Or an attorney has a scheduling conflict. Or one of the parties changes attorneys in an effort to delay. The reasons may vary but are often not sufficiently compelling to allow a child to drift in temporary care. Unfortunately, some courts have no sense of urgency when it comes to finding a permanent home for a child.

A case for bonding which employs solid research and written documentation and is presented to the court in a clear and persuasive manner can and increasingly does influence the court's decision on what is in the child's best interests.

Laws and policies have changed in the past few years, generally in favor of earlier permanence for children. ASFA puts the needs of the child at the top of the priority list. Appellate court decisions frequently recognize the importance of bonding. The average time in foster care drops from one year to the next, but far too slowly. The next chapter will review and summarize the goal: to respect bonding when it occurs and to strive for early permanence for children in care.

CHAPTER TWELVE

THE RIGHT TO A PERMANENT HOME

> *"Home is the place where, when you have to go there, they have to take you in." (Robert Frost)*

The Journey of a Foster Child

Following a complaint of abuse or neglect, the CPS (Child Protection Services) worker is required to investigate immediately. If the abuse/neglect is substantiated, four future directions or choices present themselves.

Maintaining the birth home is the first choice. Bonding is important and should be preserved when possible. Even in an unsafe and insecure home, the child is probably bonded to his or her parents. Disrupting this bond will cause additional trauma. The key to a wise decision is to consider the cost/benefit ratio. Does the cost of separation outweigh the risk to safety and security?

In-home support services can be offered. In-home trainers might teach housekeeping and parenting skills. Foster parents might be used as trainers, thus placing foster parents in the birth home rather than moving the child to the foster home.

If the child must be removed, reunification becomes the second option. Time is a critical factor and the out-of-home stay should be minimal. Caseworkers should provide birth parents with an immediate "to do" list of circumstances to remedy before the child can be returned, and then check regularly on the progress.

Sadly, twenty to forty percent of reunifications fail. Reunification may have been done without careful data-gathering and assessment. Perhaps a welfare department or court was overly biased toward biological parenthood. Maybe the reunification was done to save the state money. Whatever the reason, the failure rate is unacceptable high and the child pays the price.

Kin care is the third choice. The caseworker should undertake an immediate inventory of extended family members. If the child must be moved, and responsible willing blood relatives can be found, the child should be placed with them. Remaining with the extended family allows the child to continue close ties with known persons. The disadvantage is that kin are sometimes seen as a too-easy answer by the state and an excuse to keep birth parents and child together despite safety concerns.

When blood relatives want to foster or adopt a child in wardship, their home should be treated like any other adoptive home. Potential adoptive relatives should receive the same careful home study and scrutiny as other candidates. Kin adoptions make up 25 percent of foster children who are adopted nationally. This compares with 60 percent adopted by the foster parents and another 15 percent by non-relatives. (AFCARS, 2005)

Pseudo-Permanency Plans

Reunification and adoption are the only true permanent solutions. While ASFA (Appendix A) and the subsequent Fostering Connections Act (Appendix B) list kin care, "permanent" legal guardianship, independent living, and Another Planned Permanent Living Arrangement (APPLA) as permanency plans, they are anything but. They are pseudo-permanency plans, perhaps so-named as an excuse for our welfare and court systems at having failed children in foster care.

Kin care, especially when kin are identified immediately, can be a good temporary choice. The only way for kin care to become officially and legally permanent, however, is for the kin to adopt the child. Adoption indicates a lifetime parental commitment that mere care by relatives does not.

Permanent legal guardianship is mis-named. There is no such thing. No matter what one calls it, a guardianship can be dissolved. At best one might say that the legal guardianship is "temporarily" permanent. Legal guardianship has sometimes been offered as a permanency plan preferable to adoption by foster parents, even when the foster parents and child are bonded. Bonding is ignored while blood is given preference, genetic ties considered more binding than a history of love and nurture and habits developed.

Independent living is surely not a permanent plan. To call it such is to admit failure and give up, to agree in advance that the state cannot do what the child needs. In other words, the permanency plan is to say that a permanent home cannot be found. Very few persons, if anyone, are capable of truly living independently as an adult, certainly not our vulnerable foster children. Actually, independent living is an oxymoron. That it does not work well has been extensively demonstrated in Chapter Three. Society's resources are currently being used generously to teach so-called independent living skills. Such resources could more profitably be used to find permanent homes for older youth and to reward creative efforts to accomplish this task.

APPLA has become the new goal or plan that has replaced independent living. By making the goal vague, the illusion is created that something substantive is being done for the emancipated young adult. Discharge planning would be a far more accurate and honest term.

If the state cannot find a permanent home for every child, the state can at least be honest. Cloaking the problem with euphemisms and pseudo-permanency plans only serves to make agencies relax their efforts, believing the problem to be solved by word-play. Every child has the right to a permanent home. The only permanent lifelong solutions are reunification and adoption. The state may not be able to find permanent homes for every foster child. But at least they need to be honest and refrain from labeling other resolutions as "permanency" plans.

Conclusions

One year is a long time in the life of a child. ASFA's guidelines to achieve permanence within "child time" are critical and should be followed.

Foster care is, or should be, temporary. Foster care must not be allowed to become a way of life. Extended foster care is damaging to children.

Get started immediately. Shorten to five days the time lapse between the removal of the child and a preliminary plan with specifics for the child's return.

Inactivity on the part of the caseworker or the child's parents is not acceptable. This perpetuates extended foster care.

Reunification and adoption are the only two roads to permanence. While ASFA allows for kinship care and "permanent" legal guardianship as alternate permanency plans, they are not permanent solutions.

Concurrent planning and cooperative adoption can help avoid delays in achieving permanence. Concurrent planning provides a backup plan. Cooperative adoption allows for voluntary terminations by creating the opportunity for post-adoption contact.

Older foster children are less likely to be adopted. New ways of recruiting permanent homes for children over 10 must be found. Instead of accessing the usual pool of potential adoptive parents, ask the child who he relates to. Then contact that person.

Bonding takes precedence over kinship. Strong relationships and potential lifetime commitments are more valuable to the child than are blood ties. The marriage bond is one good example of the precedence of bonding over kinship.

Foster parents who have had the child for a year or more should be given legal standing. They have the best 24/7 knowledge of the child and are the ones most likely to adopt. They should have a voice in the arena where decisions are made.

Every child has the right to a permanent home. As ASFA makes clear, the child's rights are paramount. The primary consideration must not be the adult's right to ownership but the right of the child to a permanent home.

***

Indefinite and unmonitored foster care can generate a nightmare of angry and saddened lives, producing children and adults who take out their instability on society. Or foster care can heal and improve the lives of children, presenting society with a gift, our hope for a better future. Having

141

removed them from an abusive home, society is obliged to provide a better one. The welfare departments and courts must feel the urgency of children in vital need of safe and loving families to change ineffective laws and policies. Every child has the right to a permanent home.

APPENDICES

Summary of the Adoption and Safe Families Act of 1997
(P.L. 105-89)

Child Welfare League of America, Inc. 440 First Street. NW. Third Floor. Washington DC 20001-2085 202/638-2952

On November 19, 1997, the President signed into law (P.L. 105-89) the Adoption and Safe Families Act of 1997, to improve the safety of children, to promote adoption and other permanent homes for children who need them, and to support families. This new law makes changes and clarifications in a wide range of policies established under the Adoption Assistance and Child Welfare Act (P.L. 96-272), the major federal law enacted in 1980 to assist the states in protecting and caring for abused and neglected children. The new law:

- **Continues and Expands the Family Preservation and Support Services Program**. The Family Preservation and Support Services Program, renamed the Promoting Safe and Stable Families Program, is reauthorized through FY 2001 at the following levels: FY 1999 at $275 million; FY 2000 at $295 million; and FY 2001 at $305 million. The set-asides are maintained for the Court Improvement Program, evaluation, research, training, technical assistance, and Indian tribes. State plans are now also required to contain assurances that in administering and conducting service programs, the safety of the children to be served will be of paramount concern.

145

The new law further clarifies that for the purposes of the maintenance of effort requirement in the program, "non-federal funds" may be defined as either state or state and local funds. This change is made retroactive to the enactment of the Family Preservation and Support Services Program (P.L. 103-66) on August 10, 1993.

In addition to the funds to prevent child abuse and neglect and to assist families in crisis, the program's funds specifically include time-limited reunification services such as counseling, substance abuse treatment services, mental health services, assistance for domestic violence, temporary child care and crisis nurseries, and transportation to and from these services. Adoption promotion and support services are also included and are defined as pre- and post-adoptive services and activities designed to expedite the adoption process and support families.

- **Continues Eligibility for the Federal Title IV-E Adoption Assistance Subsidy to Children Whose Adoption is Disrupted.** Any child who was receiving a federal adoption subsidy on or after October l, 1997, shall continue to remain eligible for the subsidy if the adoption is disrupted or if the adoptive parents die.

- **Addresses Geographic Barriers to Adoption.** States are required to assure that the state will develop plans for the effective use of cross-jurisdictional resources to facilitate timely permanent placements for children awaiting adoption. The state's Title IV-E foster care and adoption assistance funding is conditioned on the state not denying or delaying a child's adoptive placement, when an approved family is available outside of the jurisdiction with responsibility for the child. Funding is also

146

conditioned upon the state granting opportunities for fair hearings for allegations of violations of the requirements. The U.S. General Accounting Office must study and report to Congress on how to improve procedures and policies to facilitate timely adoptions across state and county lines.

- **Establishes Kinship Care Advisory Panel.** HHS is required to prepare and submit, by June 1, 1999, a report for Congress on the extent of the placement of children in foster care with relatives and to convene an advisory panel on kinship care to review and comment on the report before it is submitted.

- **Issues Sense of Congress on Standby Guardianship**. It is the Sense of Congress that states should have laws and procedures to permit a parent who is chronically ill or near death to designate a standby guardian for their child, without surrendering their own parental rights. The standby guardian's authority would take effect upon the parent's death, mental incapacity, or physical debilitation and consent.

- **Establishes New Time Line and Conditions for Filing Termination of Parental Rights**. Federal law did not require states to initiate termination of parental rights proceedings based on a child's length of stay in foster care. Under the new law, states must file a petition to terminate parental rights and concurrently, identify, recruit, process and approve a qualified adoptive family on behalf of any child, regardless of age, that has been in foster care for 15 out of the most recent 22 months. A child would be considered as having entered foster care on the earlier of either the date of the first judicial finding of abuse or neglect, or 60 days after the child is removed from the home.

- **This new requirement applies to children entering foster care in the future and to children already in care.** For children already in care, states are required to phase in the filing of termination petitions beginning with children for whom the permanency plan is adoption or who have been in care the longest. One-third must be filed within six months of the end of the state's first legislative session following enactment of this law, two-thirds within 12 months and all of them within 18 months. A state must also file such a petition if a court has determined that an infant has been abandoned (as defined in state law) or if a court has determined that a parent of a child has assaulted the child, or killed or assaulted another one of their children. Exceptions can be made to these requirements if: (1) at the state's option, a child is being cared for by a relative; (2) the state agency documents in the case plan which is available for court review, a compelling reason why filing is not in the best interest of the child; or (3) the state agency has not provided to the child's family, consistent with the time period in the case plan, the services deemed necessary to return the child to a safe home.
- **Directs States to Establish Standards to Ensure Quality Services.** By January 1, 1999, states are required to develop and implement standards to ensure that children in foster care placement in public and private agencies are provided quality services that protect the safety and health of the children.
- **Requires Assessment of State Performance in Protecting Children.** HHS will develop in consultation with governors, state legislatures, state and local public officials and child welfare advocates, a set of outcome

measures to be used to assess the performance of states in operating child protection and child welfare programs to ensure the safety of children and a system for rating the performance of states with respect to the outcome measures. HHS must submit an annual report to Congress on state performance including recommendations for improvement. The first report is due May 1, 1999. Outcome measures include length of stay in foster care and number of foster placement adoptions; and, to the extent possible, are to be developed from date available from the Adoption and Foster Care Analysis and Reporting System (AFCARS).

- **Directs Development of Performance-Based Incentive Funding System.** HHS, in consultation with public officials and child welfare advocates, is required to develop and recommend to Congress a performance-based incentive system for providing payments under Title IV-B and Title IV-E of the Social Security Act by February 1999, and to submit a progress report on the feasibility, timetable and consultation process for conducting such a study by May 1998.

- **Expands Child Welfare Demonstration Waivers.** Under previous law, HHS has authority to approve up to ten child welfare demonstration waivers. Eight states (CA, DE, IL, IN, MD, NC, OH, OR) have received approval to date. This new law authorizes HHS to conduct up to 10 demonstration projects per year from FY 1998 through 2002. Specific types of demonstrations to be considered include: projects designed to identify and address reasons for delay in adoptive placements for foster children; projects designed to address parental substance abuse problems that endanger children and result in placement of a child in foster care; and projects designed to address kinship care. Eligibility for these waivers is not available if a state fails to provide health insurance coverage to any child with special needs for whom there is in effect an adoption assistance agreement.

- **Requires Study on the Coordination of Substance Abuse and Child Protection**. HHS will prepare a report which describes the extent and scope of the problem of substance abuse in the child welfare population, the types of services provided to this population and the outcomes resulting from the provision of such services, including recommendations for legislation needed to improve coordination in providing such services.

- **Authorizes the Use of the Federal Parent Locator Service.** Child welfare agencies can now use the Federal Parent Locator Service to assist in locating absent parents.

- **Extends Independent Living Services**. Young people who are no longer eligible for federal foster care assistance because their savings and assets exceed $1,000, will still be eligible for independent living services, provided their assets do not exceed $5,000.

- **Funding Source.** The provisions of this law are partially funded ($40 million over four years) from an adjustment to the $2 billion Federal Contingency Fund for State Welfare Programs, created by the 1996 welfare law (P.L. 104-193). HHS is also required to make recommendations to Congress by March 1, 1998, for improving the operation of the Contingency Fund for State Welfare Programs.

- **Effective Date:** The provisions of this new law became effective on November 19, 1997, except for the provisions dealing with termination of parental rights, disrupted adoptions, and the definition of nonfederal funds under family preservation. States have until the close of the next regular session of the state legislature to pass any state laws to comply with the new state plan requirements imposed by this law.

Fostering Connections to Success and Increasing Adoptions Act

The Fostering Connections to Success and Increasing Adoptions Act (H.R. 6893/P.L. 110-351) will help hundreds of thousands of children and youth in foster care by promoting permanent families for them through relative guardianship and adoption and improving education and health care. Additionally, it will extend federal support for youth to age 21. The act will also offer for the first time many American Indian children important federal protections and support.

With Relatives

- **Notice to Relatives When Children Enter Care.** Increases opportunities for relatives to step in when children are removed from their parents and placed in foster care by ensuring they get notice of this removal.
- **Kinship Navigator Programs.** Guarantees funds for Kinship Navigator programs, through new Family Connection grants, to help connect children living with relatives, both in and out of foster care, with the supports and assistance they need.
- **Subsidized Guardianship Payments for Relatives.** Helps children in foster care leave care to live permanently with grandparents and other relative guardians when they cannot be returned home or adopted and offers federal support to states to assist with subsidized guardianship payments to families for these children, generally to age 18. In certain circumstances, children may continue to

153

receive guardianship assistance to age 21. Clarifies that all children who, as of September 30, 2008, were receiving federally-supported subsidized guardianship payments or services in states with Child Welfare Demonstration Waivers will be able to continue to receive that assistance and services under the new program. Clarifies that children who leave foster care after age 16 for kinship guardianship are eligible for independent living services and makes them eligible for education and training vouchers.

- **Licensing Standards for Relatives.** Clarifies that states may waive non-safety related licensing standards for relatives on a case-by-case basis and requires the Department of Health and Human Services (HHS) to report to Congress on the use of licensing waivers and recommendations for increasing the percentage of relative foster family homes that are licensed.

With Adoptive Families

- **Incentives for Adoption**. Increases incentives to states to find adoptive families for children in foster care, especially those with disabilities or other special needs and older youth.
- **Adoption Assistance**. Increases opportunities for more children with special needs to receive federally-supported adoption assistance without regard to the income of the birth families from whom they were originally removed.

For further information or for a copy of a more detailed description of H.R. 6893, please contact Beth Davis-Pratt at the Children's Defense Fund at (202) 662-3629 or edavis-pratt@childrensdefense.org or Tiffany Conway at the Center for Law and Social Policy at (202) 906-8026 or tconway@clasp.org

With Birth Families and Other Relatives

- **Establishes New Family Connection Grants**. Increases resources for Kinship Navigator programs, as described above. Also provides grants for Family Group Decision-making meetings, Intensive Family Finding activities, and Residential Family-Based Substance Abuse Treatment, all of which can help children stay safely with family members and out of foster care or, once in care, return safely to their parents or find permanence with other relatives.
- **Keeping Siblings Together**. Preserves the sibling bond for children by requiring states to make reasonable efforts to place siblings together when they must be removed from their parents' home, provided it is in the children's best interests. In the case of siblings not placed together, states must make reasonable efforts to provide for frequent visitation or other ongoing interaction, unless such interaction would be harmful to any of the siblings.

Improving Outcomes for Children and Youth in Foster Care

- **Foster Care for Older Youth**. Helps youth who turn 18 in foster care without permanent families to remain in care, at state option, to age 19, 20, or 21 with continued federal support to increase their opportunities for success as they transition to adulthood.

- **Educational Stability.** Helps children and youth in foster care, guardianship and adoption achieve their educational goals by requiring that states ensure that they attend school and, when placed in foster care, they remain in their same school where appropriate, or, when a move is necessary, get help transferring promptly to a new school; also provides increased federal support to assist with school-related transportation costs.
- **Health Care Coordination.** Helps improve health care for children and youth in foster care by requiring the state child welfare agency to work with the state Medicaid agency to create a plan to better coordinate health care for these children in order to ensure appropriate screenings and assessments and follow-up treatment and to assure sharing of critical information with appropriate providers and oversight of prescription medications.

Increasing Support for American Indian and Alaska Native Children

- **Direct Access to Federal Support for Indian Tribes**. Offers, for the first time, many American Indian and Alaska Native children federal assistance and protections through the federal foster care and adoption assistance programs that hundreds of thousands of other children are eligible for already.
- **Technical Assistance and Implementation Services**. Requires HHS to provide technical assistance and implementation services dedicated to improving

services and permanency outcomes for Indian children and their families.

Improving the Quality of Staff Working with Children in the Child Welfare System

- **Extended federal support for training of staff.** Expands the availability of federal training dollars, on a phased-in basis, to reach more of those caring for and working with children in the child welfare system, including relative guardians, staff of private child welfare agencies, court personnel, attorneys, guardian ad litems, and court-appointed special advocates.

APPELLATE COURT DECISIONS FAVORING BONDING

Fortunately, courts are recognizing the importance of bonding and attachment when considering placement decisions. The courts have used terms like "continuity of care," "risks of transition," and "significant attachment" when describing the importance of attachment and keeping children in bonded relationships. Here are nine recent appellate court decisions from across the country:

Missouri

The Missouri Appellate Court upheld a ruling in favor of foster parents adopting their foster child over the objections of the child's grandparents and their Indian tribe. The child had multiple medical needs that required special medical equipment and training in its use. The foster parents became very adept at providing for the child's medical needs and a strong bond developed. Although there is a statutory preference for the child to be placed with a member of his family and tribe, the court reasoned that his foster parents' ability to provide care for his special needs and the significant emotional bond between them overrode the statutory preference. (In re C.G.L. v. McDonald County Juvenile Office, 63 S.W. 3d 693) (2002)

Kansas

The Kansas Appellate Court ruled that a lower court erred, in part, when it discounted an emotional bond between a foster child and her foster parents, which is one factor in the best interests of child. The child was placed with a foster family by the custodial agency and the agency failed to pursue adoptive placement with interested relatives. The foster family and the child's relatives both filed to adopt. The lower court had ruled that the agency initially failed in their reasonable efforts to explore adoptive placement with the relatives and, therefore, the court ruled in favor of placement with relatives. The Appellate Court affirmed the lower court ruling that the agency failed in its reasonable efforts; however, the court reversed placement with the relatives until consideration could be given to the emotional bond between the child and her foster parents in determining her best interests. (In the Interest of D.C., 32 Kan. App. 2d 962) (2004)

In a separate case, the Kansas Appellate Court ruled a lower court erred when it granted an adoption by grandparents based solely on biological preference when the foster family had more of a relationship with the child. The child had resided with his foster family for over two years when the competing petitions were filed. The court reasoned that the bond between the foster family and the child is a critical factor when determining the child's best interest. (In re Interest of J.A.,42 P. 3d 215) (2002)

Washington

The Washington Appellate Court affirmed a lower court that denied biological parents' preference to have a couple other than the family the children had been placed with to adopt. The court reasoned that the best interest of the child was to remain in the placement where he was thriving, not to undergo the risk of a transition. The record showed that the custodial family was prepared to adopt the child. They were the experienced parents of three children. The child was observed to be happy and healthy in their care and was accepted by all members of their family. At the time of the trial court's decision, the child had lived with the family for 14 of his 19 months. The trial court did not abuse its discretion by concluding that the custodial unit was the family to whom the child bonded and that he should have remained in their care. Relevant discussion as to how a court should consider placement decisions was included in the opinion.

"Evidence relevant to an adoptive placement decision may include, but is not limited to, the psychological and emotional bonds between the dependent child and its biological parents, its siblings, and its foster family; the potential harm the child may suffer if severed from contact with these persons as a result of a placement decision; the nature of the child's attachment to the person or persons constituting the proposed placement; and the effect of an abrupt and substantial change in the child's environment. An important objective is to maintain continuity in the child's relationship with a parental figure, and to avoid numerous changes in custody if this is possible without harm to the child. Where possible, the initial placement shall be viewed as the only placement for the child." (p. 13) (In re Dependency of J.S., 111 Wn. App. 796) (2002)

California

The California Appellate Court upheld a ruling in favor of continuing placement with foster parents over placement with the children's tribe. In spite of the preference for Indian children to be placed with their tribe according to the Indian Child Welfare Act, the court ruled in favor of continued placement with the children's foster parents due to their significant attachment. The court reasoned that this extraordinary emotional bond falls under the "good cause" exception to the Act. (Fresno County Dept. of Children & Family Services v. Sup..., 122 Cal. App. 4th 626) (2004)

Pennsylvania

The Pennsylvania Supreme Court ruled in favor of foster parents adopting their foster child over placement with the biological grandparents. The child was "failure to thrive" when she entered foster care and made dramatic gains while with the foster parents. The court reasoned that the risks in moving the child from the foster home where she was secure and attached were too great. (In the Interest of C.J.R., 782 A. 2d 568)(2001)

Maine

Maine's Supreme Court upheld a lower court ruling that gave adoptive placement to the foster parents over the child's grandparents. The child had lived with the foster parents for two years while the grandparents had visited infrequently. The child had many developmental delays and the foster parents had a track record of meeting her needs. The court reasoned that significant bonding occurred between the child and her foster parents, and it was in her best interest to remain with them. (In re Annie A., 2001 ME 105; similarly In re Kayla M., 2001 ME 166) (2001)

Alaska

The Alaska Supreme Court ruled for a grant of adoption of a foster child by his foster parents, while denying the biological grandparents' petition. The child had continuously resided with his foster parents from the age of seven months to three years. Although the child had a relationship with his grandparents, the court reasoned it was in the child's best interests to be adopted by his foster parents due to the significant bond with them and recognizing the child's need for "continuity of care." (In re Adoption of Bernard A., 77 P. 3d 4) (2003)

Tennessee

The Tennessee Appellate Court ruled in favor of foster parents' adoption petition over that of the child's relatives - even though it permanently separated siblings. Siblings were initially placed together in the foster home, when the youngest, a four month old, was then placed in the custody of relatives while the older one remained in the foster home. This arrangement had continued for nearly two years when the competing adoption petitions were filed. The court granted the foster parents' adoption petition of the older child thereby dismissing the relatives' petition. The relatives were able to adopt the younger child. The court reasoned that the continuity of care preference outweighed the preference for placing siblings together due to the age of the children and their respective attachment to their caregivers. (In re S.B., Tenn. App. LEXIS 308) (2000)

Indiana

The Indiana Court of Appeals recognized the importance of parenting and bonding when it comes to adoption. The Appellate Court held that biology is not more important than a child's relationship with a man who has been a father in the terms that matter most. The court upheld the adoption of a girl to a man who had cared for her as his daughter for five years while dismissing the biological aunt and uncle's adoption petition. (Gerweck v. Schoenradt, 793 N.E. 2d 1054) (2003)

Maryland

Not all higher court decisions have favored bonding. Legal precedent in Maryland has held that the rights of a biological parent cannot be terminated unless the parent is proven to be unfit at the time of the termination, or "exceptional circumstances" exist. The Maryland Court of Appeals on

January 19, 2010 (In re Adoption/Guardianship of Alonza D., Jr. and Shaydon S.) found that the best interests of the child, by itself, is not an exceptional circumstance.

"In other words, proving that a child would be better situated if parental rights were terminated is not enough to support a termination of parental rights. The specific issues in Alonza D. were whether the children's attachment to the foster parent who intended to adopt, absent proof of parental unfitness, was sufficient to terminate parental rights. The Court of Appeals said no and remanded for further proceedings."

"The Court of Appeals found that separation from the father, an asserted lack of a father-children bond, and bonding between the foster mother and the two children was not an "exceptional circumstance" sufficient to overcome the presumption that it is in the best interest of a child to maintain a relationship with the biological (natural) parent. Rather, the Court ruled that termination would require a finding based on clear and convincing evidence that "a continued parental relationship would be detrimental to the best interests of the children.""

"This decision is more than just an interesting analysis of a complex area of law. Rather, the decision focuses on the impact that the foster child-foster parent's relationship can have on a fit parent's ability to prevent an adoption. This is a common situation in foster care—involuntary removal, loss of meaningful relationship with parent, the creation of a new relationship with a foster home, a desire for permanency through a foster parent adoption, and a parent who at the time the termination decision needs to be made is not unfit and seeks to establish or reestablish the parental relationship." (Schweitzer, 2010)

Schweitzer summarizes, pointing out that the standard for termination is unfitness of the biological parent or exceptional circumstances. "The essence of the Court's ruling is that evidence that the parental relationship is detrimental to the child is a necessary ingredient of exceptional circumstances. It could be argued that a clear and convincing showing of detriment is not constitutionally required or that the need to make such a factual finding will make it much more difficult for foster parent adoptions to succeed."

The task for the trial court on remand is to define the term "detriment to the best interest of the child" in an objective way. The speculative harm that might occur upon removal from the foster home needs to be given a factual context.

First and most importantly, bonding needs to be defined in a concrete and evidentiary way. Statistics might then be presented (see Chapters Three to Six) to show the significant increase in the likelihood of dire consequences if a bonded relationship is disrupted. While neither party can predict the future with one hundred percent accuracy, the compelling statistics may raise the level of harm to the child from merely possible to more likely, and from a mere "best interest" to the level of "exceptional circumstances."

QUARTERLY SUMMARY FOR CASE CONFERENCES AND COURT HEARINGS

This summary can be used to inform the judge at a court review hearing, to update the caseworker, or simply to organize the foster parents' own thinking.

CHILD'S NAME_____ DATE _____

GENERAL: Tell what has gone on with your foster child. Mention any problems.

SCHOOL: Tell your child's grades and behavior. Attach a report card.

MEDICAL: Note any illnesses, injuries, or medical problems. Give dates of doctor visits.

DENTAL AND EYE CARE: List any dentist or optometrist visits. Give the results.

COUNSELING: List visits to the therapist and tell of your foster child's progress. Ask the therapist for a written summary.

FOSTER HOME: Tell how your child has adjusted and gotten along in your home.

SOCIAL SKILLS: Tell how your foster child has gotten along with others his or her age.

SPECIAL INTERESTS: Note any activities or hobbies that your foster child enjoys.

VISITATION: List visits with the birth family and tell how they have gone. Give facts, not your opinion.

CASEWORKER: Tell about your relationship with the child welfare department. Mention what issues you would like to discuss at the next case conference.

ANYTHING ELSE that you believe is important.

SIGNATURE OF FOSTER PARENT _____

Initial Plan for Family Reunification

The CPS case worker will complete the following plan within 24 hours of removing a child from the home and will present the plan to the parents. The purpose is to identify those specific reasons why the child was removed and allow the parents to begin immediately to work toward their child's return. This plan may be modified and expanded at the first official hearing. With this initial plan, however, parents have the immediate opportunity to demonstrate their good will.

1) **HEALTH OF BIRTH PARENT** Date to be completed: _____

____ Medical evaluation and/or treatment _____

____ Mental health evaluation and/or treatment _____

____ Drug screening _____

____ Attend AA or alcohol education classes _____

____ Other_____

2) **CHANGE OF RESIDENCE** Date to be completed:_____

____ Move to acceptable housing_____

____ Separate from abusive person_____

____ Other_____

3) **EMPLOYMENT** Date to be completed :_____

____ Show number of jobs applied for each day_____

____ Obtain a job by_____

____ Hold a job for____ week _____

____ Other _____

4) **KNOWLEDGE OF THE CHILD** Date to be completed: _____

____ Complete developmental child history _____

____ Other _____

5) **PARENT TRAINING** Date to be completed: _____

____ Classes Attended _____

____ Observation with foster parent _____

____ Volunteer time: ____ hours at daycare center_____

____ Self-taught video or computer program _____

____ Other _____

6) **VISITATION** To begin by date _____

Time? _____

Where? _____

How Often?_____

SIGNATURES:

_____

Birth parent   Caseworker

GROVES BONDING CHECKLIST (GBC)

Name_____ Birthdate _____

Caregiver's Name_____Date _____

Place the appropriate number before each listed behavior in the space provided. This data is for clinical consideration only. No cumulative score is intended.

None = 0   Some = 1   A Lot = 2

Positive Infant Behaviors (6 to 18 months)

____ Alert Appearance
____ Responds to caregiver's voice
____ Vocalizes frequently
____ Shows age-appropriate motor skills
____ Likes to be cuddled
____ Can be easily comforted by caregiver
____ Sleeps well
____ Eats well
____ Prefers primary caregiver over others

Negative Infant Behaviors

____ Cries or is fussy most of the time
____ Resistant to comforting
____ Overly demanding
____ Delayed developmental milestones
____ Stiffens or is rigid when held
____ Flat or empty emotion
____ Lacks age-appropriate motor skills

Positive Pre-School Checklist (18-60 months)

____ Explores surroundings
____ Enjoys hugs and physical contact with main caregivers
____ Copies mannerisms of main caregivers
____ Physical development at age-appropriate levels
____ Makes eye contact
____ Shows responses to separation from caregivers
____ Able to set limits on own behavior (age 3+)
____ Shows some understanding of how others feel
____ Comfortable enough to get in and out of caregiver's lap

Negative Pre-School Checklist

____ Resistant to comforting and nurturing
____ Fails to imitate behavior
____ Overly affectionate to strangers.
____ Does not appear relaxed or happy
____ Fails to show normal fears.

Positive School-Age Checklist (5-12)

____ Makes eye contact appropriately
____ Comfortable around primary caregivers
____ Gets along with friends
____ Shows appropriate responses to situations
____ Avoids self-harm and dangerous situations
____ Accepts comfort when in pain
____ Plays with peers without hurting them
____ Understands consequences of bad behavior
____ Sees self as a member of the family
____ Perceived by friends, school, and neighbors as a member
of the caregiver's family

Negative School-Age Checklist

_____ Fails to make eye contact
_____ Cruel to animals
_____ Destroys property
_____ Steals
_____ Poor relationships with peers
_____ Lies about things that are obvious
_____ Makes inappropriate demands
_____ Overly dependent or clingy
_____ Few or no friends

A DAILY JOURNAL FOR FOSTER PARENTS

How Does This Benefit the Parent?

- Keeping a daily journal is the number one way foster parents can prepare for case conferences and/or help their attorney make their case in court. Judges can make decisions about a child's case plan only based on what is presented in court.
- The book is a handy reminder to keep regular notes on their foster child. In addition, it includes much valuable information in the Appendices.
- Foster parents can use the journal to record school reports, medical and counseling appointments, good and bad behavior, and to document any controversies or allegations.

Key Features

- Contains simple instructions on how to keep a journal, what and what not to put in, and ample space for daily notes.
- Quarterly outlines for summarizing information for case conferences and court hearings.
- An inside-cover pocket to hold receipts for reimbursable expenses.
- An Appendix with critical information on discipline, life books, treating the detached child, how to prevent and survive allegations, and many other important issues on foster care and adoption.

- The cover and appendices can be customized to meet the wishes of any public or private agency. Specific forms and policies can be added.

Cost

Single copies of the Daily Journal are inexpensive. The cost goes down considerably with orders of 50 copies or more.

More Information

Access the ACT website at www.adoptioninchildtime.org

To Order

Please call 800-705-7526 or email fosterjournal@schooldatebooks.com for more information about customizing your journal and/or to order. Ask for Paul.

REFERENCES

"Abused, Abandoned Juveniles Get Schooled for Adult Life." (1996) San Diego Daily Transcript. (October 17).

Adoption and Safe Families Act (ASFA) (1997) US Congress.

Adoption and Foster Care Analysis Reporting System (AFCARS).

Adoption in Child Time (ACT) www.adoptioninchildtime.org.

Ainsworth, M. (1967) Infancy in Uganda: Infant care and the growth of love. Baltimore: Johns Hopkins Press.

Ainsworth, M. (1993) Attachments and other affectional bonds across the life cycle. Ch. 2 in Marris, P. Attachment across the Life Cycle. New York: Routledge.

Aldgate, Jane. (1994) Graduating from care: a missed opportunity for encouraging successful citizenship. In Children & Youth Services Review, special issue: Preparing foster youth for adulthood, Vol. 16(3-4), 255-272.

Alexander, G. and Huberty, T. (1993) Caring for Troubled Children: The Villages Follow-up Study. Bloomington, IN: The Villages of Indiana.

American Academy of Pediatrics. (2008) Understanding the emotional and behavioral consequences of child abuse. Clinical report. Vol. 121. Number 3. September.

American Academy of Pediatrics. (2000) Committee on early childhood, adoption, and dependent care. Developmental issues for young children in foster care. Pediatrics. 106(5) 1145-50.

Arredondo, David and Edwards, Leonard (2000) Attachment, bonding, and reciprocal connectedness: Limitations of attachment theory in the juvenile and family court. Journal of the Center for Families, Children, and the Courts. pp. 109-127.

Azar, B. (1995) Foster care has a bleak history. Washington, DC: American Psychological Association. November.

Barden, J.C. (1991) After release from foster care, many turn to lives on the street: They lack simple skills to make it on their own. New York Times, Jan 6.

Barrett, Paula and Holmes, Jane (2001) Attachment Relationships as Predictors of Cognitive Interpretation and Response Bias in Late Adolescence. New York: Human Sciences Press, Inc.

Barth, R.P (1986) Emancipation services for adolescents in foster care. National Association of Social Workers, Inc.

Barth, R.P (1990) On their own: The experience of youth after foster care. Child and Adolescent Social Work Journal, Vol. 7(5), 419-446.

Barth, R.P, Wildfire, J.; and Green, R. (2006) Placement into foster care and the interplay of urbanicity, child behavior problems, and poverty. American Journal of Orthopsychiatry, Vol. 76, No. 3, pp. 358-366.

Bassuk, Ellen L. et al. (1997) Homelessness in female-headed families: Childhood and adult risk and protective factors. American Journal of Public Health, Vol. 87(2), Feb, 241-248.

Bayles, F. (1995) Onslaught of problems threatens nation's foster care system. Los Angeles Times, May 7.

Berger, K. (2001) The Developing Person through the Life Span. New York: Worth.

Blankertz, L., Cnaan, R., and Freedman, E. (1993) Childhood risk factors in dually diagnosed homeless adults. Social Work, Vol. 38(5), Sept, 587-596.

Belsky, J and Nazowrski, T (1998) Clinical Implications of Attachment. Hillsdale, N.J.: Erlbaum.

Bond, M. & Bond, S. (2007) Review of attachment and bonding: A new synthesis. Journal of Nervous and Mental Disease. Vol. 195, No. 8, pp. 711-712.

Bontrager, M. and Kenny, J (2004) Pseudo-bonding and other myths. Fostering Families Today, July/August, pp. 41-44.

Bowlby, J (1969) Attachment and Loss. Vol. 1. Attachment (1982, 2nd ed) London and New York: Hogarth.

Bowlby, J. (1973) Attachment and Loss. Vol. 2, Separation, Anxiety and Anger. London and New York: Hogarth. p. 279.

Bowlby, J. (1979) The Making and Breaking of Affectional Bonds. London: Tavistock. p. 41, pp.71-72, p. 77, p.130.

Bowlby, J (1988) A Secure Base, Parent-Child Attachment and Healthy Human Development. New York: Basic Books.

Brody, S (1993) The Concepts of Attachment and Bonding. In T. Cohen et al (eds.) The Vulnerable Child, Vol. 1, Madison, CT: International Universities Press, Inc.

Burton, John (2006) Supporting THP-Plus for California's Emancipated Foster Youth: A Compilation of Statistics. Every Child Foundation.

Bush, Rose (2001) Bonding and Attachment. Prescott, AZ: Bush Publishing. p. 18.

Cahn, Katharine and Johnson, Paul. (1993) Children can't wait. Washington DC: Child Welfare League of America.

California League of Women Voters. (1998) Education Fund. Juvenile Justice Study Committee. July.

Calsyn, R., and Roades, L. (1994) Predictors of past and current homelessness. Journal of Community Psychology, Vol. 22(3), Jul, 272-278.

Carter, C. et al (eds.) (2005) Attachment and Bonding: A New Synthesis. MA: MIT Press.

Casey, Jim (2005) The Casey Young Adult Survey: Findings Over Three Years. Casey Family Programs - Fostering Families, Fostering Change.

Casey, Jim (2007) Time for Reform: Aging Out and On Their Own- More Teens Leaving Foster Care Without a Permanent Family. Jim Casey Youth Opportunities Initiative.

Cassidy, Jude and Shaver, Phillip (1999) Handbook of Attachment: Theory, Research, and Clinical Applications. New York: The Guilford Press.

Cauce, A. et al. (1998) Homeless youth in Seattle. Youth characteristics, mental health needs, and intensive case management. In Epstein, Michael H. Ed, Outcomes for children and youth with emotional and behavioral disorders and their families: Programs and evaluation best practices. Austin, TX: Pro-Ed, Inc, xviii, p. 738.

Chestang, L. and Heyman, I. (1973) "Reducing the length of foster care." Social Work. Jan.

Child Welfare Information Gateway. (2008) Postadoption contact agreements between birth and adoptive families. Retrieved on 2-15-10.

Citizen's Committee for Children of New York, Inc. (1984) The foster care exit - ready or not: An inquiry into how New York City prepares children in foster care for discharge to independent living. p. 41.

Clark, H. et al. (1998) An individualized wraparound process for children in foster care with emotional/behavioral disturbances: follow-up findings and implications from a controlled study. In Epstein, Michael H. Ed, Outcomes for children and youth with emotional and behavioral disorders and their families: Programs and evaluation best practices. Austin, TX: Pro-Ed, Inc, xviii, 513.

Coalition for the Homeless. (1989) Blueprint for solving New York's homeless crisis. New York City: A Report to Mayor David Dinkins. p. 101.

Cohen, Theodore et al. (1993) The Vulnerable Child. CN: International Universities Press, Inc.

Cole, Susan (2005) Foster caregiver motivation and infant attachment: How do reasons for fostering affect relationships? Child and Adolescent Social Work Journal, Vol. 22.

Conlan, Roberta, ed. (1999) States of Mind: New Discoveries about How Our Brains Make Us Who We Are. New York: Wiley. p. 7.

Cook, Ronna J. (1994) Are we helping foster care youth prepare for their future? Children and Youth Services Review, Vol 16, Nov. 3-4, 213-229.

Courtney, Mark and Piliavin, Irving. (1998) Foster youth transitions to adulthood: Outcomes 12 to 18 months after leaving out-of-home care. U of Wisconsin, Madison: School of Social Work and Institute for Research on Poverty.

Courtney, M., Piliavin, I., Grogan-Kaylor, A. and Nesmith, A. (2001) Foster youth transitions to adulthood: A longitudinal study of youth leaving care. Child Welfare, 80, 685-717.

Courtney, M., Terao, S., and Bost, N. (2004) Midwest Evaluation of the Adult Functioning of Former Foster Youth: Conditions of Youth Preparing to Leave State Care. Chapin Hall Center for Children at the University of Chicago.

Davis, L. and Winkleby, M. (1993) Sociodemographic and health-related risk factors among African-American,

Caucasian and Hispanic homeless men: a comparative study. Journal of Social Distress and the Homeless. Vol 2, No 2.

Desai, R., J. Lam, and R. Rosenheck. (2000) Childhood risk factors for criminal justice involvement in a sample of homeless people with serious mental illness. Journal of Nervous & Mental disease, Vol 188(6) Jun, 324-332.

Diagnostic and Statistical Manual of Mental Disorders. 4th edition (DSM-IV). (1994) Washington DC: American Psychiatric Association.

Doll, Edgar (1965) Vineland Social Maturity Scale. Circle Pines, MN: American Guidance Service, Inc.

Doyle, Joseph J Jr.(2007) Child Protection and Adult Crime: Using Investigator Assignment to Estimate Causal Effects of Foster Care. NBER Working Paper No. 13291.

Dozier, Mary et al (2001) Attachment for infants in foster care. Child Development. 72: 1467-77. p. 502.

Erikson, Erik. (1950) Childhood and Society. New York: Norton.

Erikson, Erik. (1968) Identity: Youth and Crisis. New York: Norton.

Fahlberg, Vera (1979) Attachment and Separation - Putting the Pieces Together. Chelsea, MI: Department of Social Services. p. 7, pp. 42-44.

Fahlberg, V. (1991) A child's journey through placement. Indianapolis: Perspectives Press.

Fanshel, D., Finch, S., and Grundy, J. (1989) Foster children in life-course perspective: the Casey Family Program Experience. Child Welfare, Vol. 68(5), Sept-Oct, 467-478.

Feeney, J.; Passmore, N.; and Peterson, C. (2007) Adoption, attachment, and relationship concerns: A study of adult adoptees. Personal Relationships. Vol. 14, No. 1, pp.129-147.

Foster Care Youth United. (1994) Speak out: If you left foster care tomorrow, what would be your biggest worry? A publication of Youth Communications New York Center, Inc. New York, May/June.

Foster Parent Daily Journal. (2008). Lafayette, IN: School Datebooks. www.adoptioninchildtime.org

Fowler, Patrick, Toro, Paul, and Miles, Bart (2009) American Journal of Public Health, Vol., 99, No. 8.

Freedman, D. and Hemenway. D. (2000) Precursors of lethal violence: a death row sample. Social Science & Medicine, Vol. 50(12), Jun, 1757-1770.

Frost, R (2002) The Death of the Hired Man. The Poetry of Robert Frost. New York, Holt.

Furstenberg, F. and M. Hughes (1995) Social capital and successful development among at-risk youth. Journal of Marriage and the Family. 57, 580-592.

Gaunt, Tom and Jean. (2008) Why and how to prepare a life book. In: Foster Parent Daily Journal. Lafayette, IN: School Datebooks.

Goldstein, J., Freud, A., and Solnit, A. (1973) Beyond the Best Interests of the Child. New York; International U.

Goulet, C., Bell, L., Tribble, D., Paul, D., and Lang, A. (1998) A concept analysis of parent-infant attachment. Journal of Advanced Nursing, Vol. 28, No. 5, pp. 1071-1081.

Greenberg, Mark T (1999) Attachment and psychopathology in childhood. In J. Cassidy and P. R. Shaver (Eds.). Handbook of attachment: Theory, research, and clinical applications (pp. 469-496). New York: Guilford.

Grigsby, Kevin. (1994) Maintaining attachment relationships among children in foster care. Families in Society. Vol. 75, No. 5.

Groves, Lori and Kenny, James (2009) The high cost of emancipation. Fostering Families Today. March/April.

Groves, Lori and Kenny, James (2010) The right to a permanent home. Fostering Families Today. January/February.

Haapasalo, Jaana. (2000) Young offenders' experiences of child protection services. Journal of Youth & Adolescence, Vol. 29(3), June, 355-371.

Herman, D. et al. (1997) Adverse childhood experiences: Are they risk factors for adult homelessness? Am J Public Health, 87:249-255.

Hirschi, Travis. (1969) Causes of Delinquency. Los Angeles, CA: University of California Press.

Holmes, J. (1996) Attachment, Intimacy, Autonomy. New Jersey and London: Aronson.

Honig, A. (2002) Secure relationships: Nurturing infant/toddler attachment in early care settings. Washington, DC: National Association for the Education of Young Children.

Honoring Emancipated Youth (2005) Barriers Facing Foster Care Youth: National and Local Statistics about Emancipating Foster Youth. Retrieved on Nov. 22, 2009, From www.heysf.org

Hughes, D. (1997) Facilitating Developmental Attachment: The Road to Emotional Recovery and Behavioral Change in Foster and Adopted Children. New Jersey and London: Aronson.

Hughes, D. (2006) Building the Bonds of Attachment: Awakening Love in Deeply Troubled Children. New York: Aronson.

Indiana Child Welfare Manual (Revised 2000) Section 805:12.

Iwaniec, Dorota (2006) The Child's Journey Through Care: Placement Stability, Care Planning, and Achieving Permanency. Belfast: Queen's University. p. 49.

Jencks, Christopher. (1994) The Homeless. Cambridge, MA: Harvard University Press.

John, Jaiya (2008) Beautiful. Silver Spring, MD: Soul Water Rising. p. 28.

Judicial Education Center. Institute of Public Law. (1997-2010) Child Welfare Handbook. Retrieved on 2/3/2010, from http://jec.unm.edu/resources/benchbooks/child_law/intro.htm

Karen, R. (1994) Becoming Attached. New York: Warner. p. 58.

Katz, Jeff. (2009) Adoption scandal: Interstate barriers keep kids in foster care. The Huffington Post. (Downloaded 2-6-10).

Keck, G. and Kupecky, R (1995) Adopting the Hurt Child. Colorado Springs: Pinon.

Kenny, Peter. (2008) How to keep a journal. In: Foster Parent Daily Journal. Lafayette, IN: School Datebooks.

Kenny, J (1965) Interviewing relatives through questionnaires. Mental Hospitals, April, pp. 121-123.

Kenny, J., Pryor, B., and Watson-Duvall, D. (1995) Cooperative adoption: One solution to foster care drift. Adoptalk. Winter.

Kenny, J (2001) What Happens When Bonded Relationships Are Interrupted? See Legal Resource Center at adoptioninchildtime.org

Ketcham, O. (1998) Parental laws must put children first. The Sacramento Bee, p. B9.

Kingsley, Emily (2009) Juveniles and status offenses: The impact of Hirschi's bonds on juvenile delinquency. Journal of Offender Rehabilitation, Vol. 23, pp. 117-129.

Klaus, M. and Kennell, J. (1976) Maternal-Infant Bonding: The Impact of Early Separation or Loss on Family Development. St. Louis: Mosby.

187

Klaus, M., and Kennell, J. (1982) Parent-Infant Bonding (2nd). St Louis: Mosby.

Klaus, M., Kennell, J., and Klaus, P. (1995) Bonding: Building the Foundations of Secure Attachment and Independence. Reading, MA: Addison-Wesley.

Kobak, R. (1999) Separation and the Emotional Dynamics of Attachment. In Cassidy, J. & Shaver, P. (Eds.) Handbook of Attachment (pp. 88-105) New York: Guilford Press.

Kobak, R., Little, M., Race, E., and Acosta, M. (2001) Attachment disruptions in seriously emotionally disturbed children: Implications for treatment. Attachment and Human Development. Vol. 3. No. 3. December.

Koegel P., Melamid, E. and BurnamM. (1995) Childhood risk factors for homelessness among homeless adults. Am J Public Health, 85:1642-1649.

Kulp, J. (1993) Families at Risk. Minneapolis: Better Endings. p. 214.

Lloyd, C. (1998) Risk factors for problem drug use: Identifying vulnerable groups. Drugs: Education, Prevention & Policy, Vol. 5(3), Nov, 217-232.

Main, M. (1996) Introduction to the special section on attachment and psychopathology: Overview of the field of attachment. Journal of Consulting and Clinical Psychology, 64(2), 237-43.

Mangine, S. et al. (1990) Homelessness among adults raised as foster children: A survey of drop-in center users. Psychological Reports, Vol. 67(3 Pt1), Dec, 739-45.

Margetson, N. and C. Lipman. (1990) Children at risk: the impact of poverty, the family and street on homeless and runaway youth in New York City. Presentation delivered at the National Symposium on Youth Victimization, Apr 27. New York: Covenant House.

Marvin, R. and Britner, P. (1999) Normative development: the ontogeny of attachment. In Cassidy, J. and Shaver, P. (eds.), Handbook of attachment theory and research. New York: Guilford Press. p. 65.

Maslow, Abraham. (1943) A theory of human motivation. Psychological Review. 50, 370-396.

McDonald, T., et al. (1993) Assessing the long-term effects of foster care: a research synthesis. Madison, WI: Institute for Research on Poverty.

McEwen, Bruce. (2007) Stress and the Brain. In States of Mind. R. Conlan, ed. New York: Wiley.

McWey, L. (2004) Predictors of attachment styles of children in foster care: An attachment theory model for working with families. Journal of Marriage and Family Therapy. Vol. 30, No. 4.

Mercer, R. (1990) Parents at Risk. New York: Springer Publishing Co.

Miller, Warren and Rodgers, Joseph (2001) The Ontogeny of Human Bonding Systems- Evolutionary Origins, Neural Bases, and Psychological Manifestations. Boston: Kluwer Academic Publishers.

Monck, E., Reynolds, J., and Wigfall, V. (2003) The Role of Concurrent Planning: Making Permanent Placements for Young Children. London: British Association for Adoption and Fostering.

Mooney, C. (2010) Theories of Attachment. An Introduction to Bowlby, Ainsworth, Gerber, Brazelton, Kennell, and Klaus. St. Paul, MN: Redleaf Press.

Mortenson, Greg and Relin, David (2006) Three Cups of Tea: One Man's Mission to Promote Peace...One School at a Time. New York: Penguin.

Moss, K. (2009) What is Attachment? Association for Treatment and Training in the Attachment of Children.

Retrieved on 10/21/09, from http://www.attach.org/whatisattachment.htm

National Association of Social Workers. (1991) Finding from a national survey of shelters for runaway and homeless youth: executive summary of key NASW survey findings. Survey supported by the U.S. Department of Health and Human Services. Grant number 90K2124.

National Commission on Family Foster Care. (1991) A Blueprint for Fostering Infants, Children, and Youths in the 1990's. Washington DC: Child Welfare League of America.

Nazario, Sonia (1993) When Cries For Help Go Unheard. Los Angeles Times.

Newton, R., Litrownik, A., and Ladsverk, J. (2000) Children and youth in foster care: Disentangling the relationship between problem behaviors and number of placements. Child Abuse & Neglect, Vol. 24, pp.1363-1374.

Nichols, William, Pace-Nichols, Mary Anne, and Associates (2009) Handbook of Family Development and Intervention. Wilby Series in Couples and Family Dynamics.

O'Brien, Pat. (1993) Youth homelessness and the lack of adoption planning for older children. Adoptalk, Spring.

Pardeck, John T (1984) Multiple placement of children in foster family care: An empirical analysis. National Association of social Workers. November/December Issue. p. 508.

Parker, G (1990) The parental bonding instrument. Social Psychiatry and Psychiatric Epidemiology, 25, 281-282.

Parkes, C., Stevenson-Hinde, J., and Martin, P. (eds.) (1993) Attachment across the Life Cycle. London and New York: Routledge.

Pecora, Peter et al. (2005) Improving family foster care: Findings from the Northwest Foster Care Alumni Study. Seattle, WA: Casey Family Programs.

Perry, Bruce. (2010) Bonding and attachment in maltreated children: Consequences of emotional neglect in childhood. Adapted in part from: Maltreated children: Experience, brain development and the next generation. New York: Norton (in preparation).

Pew Commission (2004) Pew Commission Report on Foster Care Drift. Fostering Families Today, May/June, pp. 18-19.

Piliavin, I. et al. (1993) The duration of homeless careers: an exploratory study. Chicago IL: Social Service Review.

Presidential Initiative (2008) Youth Aging Out of Foster Care Identifying Strategies and Best Practices.

Prior, Vivien & Glaser, Danya (2006) Understanding Attachment and Attachment Disorders-Theory, Evidence, and Practice. London and Philadelphia: Jessica Kingsley.

Randolph, Elizabeth (1997) Randolph Attachment Disorder Questionnaire. Evergreen, CO: The Attachment Center Press.

Rohter, Larry. (1992) To save or end a troubled parent's rights. New York Times, 10/4, Vol 142 Issue 49109, Section 4.

Roman, N. and Wolfe, P. (1995) Web of failure: The relationship between foster care and homelessness. Public Welfare, Winter, Vol. 55(1), 4.

Rosenheck, Robert and Fontana, Alan. (1994) A model of homelessness among male veterans of the Vietnam war generation. American Journal of Psychiatry, Vol. 151(3), Mar, 421-427.

Rossi, Alice and Rossi, Peter (1990) Of Human Bonding, Parent-Child Relations Across the Life Course. New York: Aldine de Gruyter.

Ryan, J., Testa, M. and F. Zhai. (2008) African-American youth in foster care and the risk of delinquency: The value of social bonds and permanence. Child Welfare, 87, 115-140.

Ryan, Joseph, Hernandez, Pedro, and Herz, Denise (2007) Developmental trajectories of offending for male adolescents leaving foster care. Social Work Research. Vol. 31, No. 2, pp. 83-93.

Samuels, Gina (2008) A Reason, A Season, or a Lifetime of Relational Permanence among Adults with Foster Care Backgrounds. U. of Chicago: Chapin Hall Center for Children.

Schofield, Gillian (2002) The significance of a secure base: A psychosocial model of long-term foster care. Child and Family Social Work, Vol. 7, pp. 259-272.

Schweitzer, H. (2010) The rights of foster children. Legal update. In James R. Marsh, ChildLaw blog. March 11.

Shaffer, D., and Caton, C. (1984) Runaway and homeless youth in New York City. Study funded by a grant from the Ittleson Foundation and the New York State Office of Mental Health. p. 57.

Shirk, M. and Stangler, G. (2004) On Their Own: What Happens to Kids When They Age Out of the Foster Care System? Cambridge, MA: Basic Books.

Shlay, Anne and Rossi, Peter (1992) Social science research and contemporary studies of homelessness. Annual Review of Sociology, Vol. 18, 129-160.

Singer, Elly; Doornenbal, Jeannette; & Okma, Krista (2004) Why do children resist or obey their foster parents? The inner logic of children's behavior during discipline. Child Welfare League of America. Nov/Dec, Vol. 83, No. 6.

Steinhauer, P. (1991) The Least Detrimental Alternative. Toronto: U of Toronto. p. 23, p. 82.

Stokes, J., and Strothman, L. (1996) The use of bonding studies in child welfare permanency planning. Child & Adolescent Social Work Journal. Vol. 13, No. 4.

Strijker, Johan, Knorth, Erik, and Knot-Dickscheit, Jana (2008) Placement history of foster children: A study of placement history and outcomes in long-term family foster care. Child Welfare League of America.

Study of Runaway Youths Finds One-Third Were in Foster Care. (1992) St. Louis Post-Dispatch, January.

Sumerlin, John (1999) Cognitive-affective preparation for homelessness: quantitative and qualitative analysis of childhood out-of-home placement and child abuse in a sample of homeless men. Psychological Reports. Vol 85(2), Oct, 553-573.

Susser, Ezra et al. (1991) Childhood antecedents of homelessness in psychiatric patients. American Journal of Psychiatry. Vol 148(8), Aug, 1026-1030.

Teggart, Tom (2006) The Child's Journey Through Care: Placement Stability, Care Planning, and Achieving Permanency. New York: Wiley (Chapter 9).

Tern, Melanie (1985) The leap of faith: Claiming and bonding in adoption. Paper presented at the North American Council on Adoptable children's conference in Albuquerque, NM.

Thorpe, R. (1980) The experiences of children and parents living apart: implications and guidelines for practice. In Triseliotis (ed.) New Developments in Foster Care and Adoption, pp. 85-100. London: Routledge.

Triseliotis, J. (1980) Growing up in foster care and after. In J. Triseliotis (ed.), New Developments in Foster Care and Adoption, pp. 131-161. London: Routledge.

Triseliotis, J. (1983) Identity and security in adoption and long-term fostering, British Agencies for Adoption and Fostering. 7(1), 22-23.

U.S. Department of Justice, Bureau of Justice Statistics (2005) Corrections at a Glance: Retrieved on November 25, 2008, from www.ojp.usdoj.gov/bjs/correct.htm.

Westat, Inc. (1991) A national evaluation of Title IV-E foster care independent living programs for youth. Phase II, final report, Vols. I & II, Rockville, MD: Westat, Inc.

Whiting, J. and Lee, R. (2003) Voices from the system: A qualitative study of foster children's stories. Family Relations. Vol. 52, No. 3.

Wilmshurst, Linda (2003) Child & Adolescent Psychopathology: A Casebook. Sage Publications, Thousand Oaks.

Winkleby, M. and Fleshin, D. (1993) Physical, addictive and psychiatric disorders among homeless veterans and no veterans. Public Health Report, Vol. 108, No. 1.

Winkleby, M. and White, R. (1992) Homeless adults without apparent medical and psychiatric impairment: onset of morbidity over time. Hospital and Community Psychiatry, Vol. 43, No. 10.

www.childrensrights.org   Children's Rights – Foster Children.

www.heysf.org Hey Publications on Foster Care.

Zlotnick, C., Kronstadt, D., and Klee, L. (1998)   Foster care children and family homelessness. American Journal of Public Health. Vol. 88:9, Sept., p. 1368.

James Kenny is a clinical psychologist in private practice in Rensselaer, Indiana with doctorates in psychology and anthropology, as well as a master's degree in social work. He has taught at several major universities and has been the director of a child guidance clinic and a mental health center. With his wife he is the author of "Whole Life Parenting, Happy Parenting, Making the Family Matter" and other books and articles. He is the founder of "Adoption in Child Time" (ACT) and a board member of "Fostering Families Today" magazine. The Kenny's are the parents of biological, adopted, and foster children. Jim loves to run, read, write, and tell stories.

 Lori Groves has a master's degree in Marriage an Family Therapy. She has authored several articles in "Fostering Families Today." Lori is also on the board of directors for "Adoption in Child Time" (ACT). The Groves' are the parents of biological, adopted, and foster children. Lori loves to read, scrapbook, and ride motorcycles.

Made in the USA
Charleston, SC
20 May 2010